10

MINUTE GUIDE TO

THE STOCK MARKET

by Dian Vujovich

alpha
books

A Division of Macmillan General Reference
A Simon & Schuster Macmillan Company
1633 Broadway, New York, NY 10019-6705

Publisher Theresa Murtha
Managing Editor Michael Cunningham
Editor Dick Staron
Production Editor Phil Kitchel
Cover Designer Dan Armstrong
Designer Glenn Larsen
Indexer Sandy Henselmeier
Production Team Angela Calvert, Janelle Herber, Mary Hunt, Malinda Kuhn, Beth Rago

CONTENTS

INTRODUCTION

Welcome to the world of stocks!

If you picked this book up, you must have some curiosity about that six-letter word that has made some people millionaires over the years and caused others to take their own lives.

Stocks and the stock market are like capitalism's own "Wheel of Fortune." But before you decide to participate in this weekday event, it's best to know a little bit about what makes a company tick and how stocks are brought to market.

In the *10 Minute Guide to the Stock Market*, you'll learn all about the basics of stocks and the stock market beginning with how the markets have evolved and where money came from, right on down to investment strategies and how to place your stock orders.

You'll also learn about the different types of stock, what the difference between asset allocation and diversification is, and when to sell your stocks. There's even a chapter on mutual funds.

The 20 lessons in this book are designed to quickly acquaint you with some of the most common aspects of the stock market, familiarize you with the industry's jargon, and provide you with the groundwork from which your knowledge of stocks and the stock market can begin to grow.

Obviously, there is much more to stocks and the markets than can be addressed in this little book. But the *10 Minute Guide to the Stock Market* isn't supposed to be a stock encyclopedia. It's supposed to be a primer.

With that in mind, enjoy the journey. The world of equities is one of the most fruitful, ever-changing, and exciting dimensions of our country's fabric. It's also one that speaks to the consumer products that we use, the cars that we drive, the foods that we eat, the medicines we take, and the banks that we rely on.

Aside from the sunshine, moonlight, and air that we breathe, an awful lot of everything else you come in contact with in the course of a day is made or manufactured by someone other than you. And that someone, more often than not, represents a company that you could be investing in.

The *10 Minute Guide to the Stock Market* will get you started on that investing road.

Acknowledgements

Few things in life are ever accomplished alone. My thanks to Alwyn Taylor, Ben Hillard, Keith Bush, and Phil Keating for their support and direction.

1

WELCOME TO THE WORLD OF STOCKS

In this lesson, you will learn about the origin of money and how stocks first originated.

STOCKS ARE PART OF DAILY LIFE

You'd have to be from another planet not to have at least heard about the stock market these days. Every day of the week there are more TV and radio reports, more newsletters and financial magazines, and more securities salespeople and money professionals talking about what's happening on Wall Street than ever in the history of the securities trading. But things haven't always been that way.

Americans have been trading stocks since the late 1700s, but as recently as 40 years ago, stocks were thought by the experts to be too risky an investment for the average person. That opinion was based, in part, on the fact that it took 25 years for the Dow Jones Industrial Average to return to the record high level it reached before the Crash of 1929.

So, while hearing or reading about stocks is one thing, actually understanding what stocks—and the stock markets—are all about is quite another.

If you're new to the world of equities (*equities* is the plural form of *equity*, another way to say *stock*), learning how the stock markets work is best understood by first looking at money and its origins, and then understanding that perceptions play as big a role in the markets as stocks themselves.

Equity   Another way of referring to stock, or the ownership right that shareholders in a company possess.

Stock   1) The ownership of a corporation that's represented by shares. Each share of stock has a stake in the corporation's earnings and assets, the value of which typically changes over time. 2) Another way of referring to the inventory in a store or manufacturing plant.

WHERE MONEY CAME FROM

Long before people exchanged dollar bills and coins for CD-ROMS and four-wheel drives, or a Coca-Cola and hamburger, they bartered for the goods and services they needed. You exchanged a few bales of cotton for a cow. As villages around the globe developed from tiny hamlets into larger communities and then cities, bartering became difficult and time consuming, and finding someone to barter with was often cumbersome.

Probably the first use of coins and paper notes was in Mesopotamia, what we now refer to as southern Iraq, some 4,500 years ago.

The use of coins made out of metals such as gold, silver, or copper as a means of paying for goods and services can be traced back as far as 2500 B.C. And, during the 7th century B.C., the kingdom of Lydia, now Turkey, began minting coins. The Chinese, in the 11th century, first introduced paper money.

Today, the money we use in the U.S. is considered a *fiat currency* because it has no intrinsic value. Dollar bills, pennies, nickels, dimes, and quarters can't be exchanged for gold or silver; they merely represent the currency of our country. That means the value of money is in the eye of the beholder and not in what is backing the currency itself.

THE FIRST STOCKS

Making money before the securities markets were created was done in basically two ways: 1) Some people used their disposable income to buy goods and sell them at higher prices, thereby making money from the sale of those trades. 2) Others learned that money could be loaned, and the borrower paid a fee—or interest—for the use of that money. The notion of *investment capital* first began in the money handling of the latter group.

Some of the earliest recorded stock transactions came as a result of financing the War of Spanish Succession. That financing move led to what historians called the South Sea Bubble, a hugely popular and highly speculative investment craze. Here's what happened.

In 1711, the London securities market floated government debt issues to help finance that war. Because people had little faith in the government's ability to repay its debt obligation, the bonds they issued could be exchanged for shares of the South Sea Company, a company that hoped to make its money trading with India.

Because the bonds issued could be converted to stock, at much higher prices than the bonds originally cost, sales were hot. So hot that investors began gobbling up not only those securities but almost any kind of stock available on Exchange Alley, London's securities market at the time.

The buying frenzy led to financial disaster for most individuals and the coining of the term "South Sea Bubble." The "bubble," which burst, refers to over-zealous investors with exceptionally out-of-line expectations.

Investors in America missed their opportunity to join in the South Sea Bubble craze simply because there were no real securities trading markets in the U.S. at the time of the craze. It took until the 1790s before a U.S. stock market was created in New York City. And in 1792, a stock market crash occurred.

PERCEPTIONS

Three lessons can be learned from the history of the stock markets:

1. Emotions can and often do play a big part in the stock choices people make.

2. Not all stocks make money.

3. Investing is risky business.

With that in mind, it's best to keep a cool head and exercise some thoughtful evaluation before buying your first shares of stock.

 Creating Wealth   The road to riches for stock investors does not now, nor has it ever, followed a straight line upwards.

In this lesson, you learned the history of the stock market and some of the risks involved in stocks.

WHO OWNS STOCKS?

In this lesson, you will learn about the people and the different institutions who own stocks.

Stocks are owned by literally everybody. People just like you and me, little old ladies, young kids, old men, brand-new and well-established institutions, insurance companies, pension funds, mutual funds, banks, churches, the employed, the unemployed, the retired, and the list goes on and on.

Surveys showing stock ownership typically break the who-owns-stocks question into two categories—*households* and *institutions*.

Household According to the Federal Reserve, a "household" is not just limited to individuals; it also includes entities such as non-profit organizations, unit investment trusts, churches, and other categories not accounted for elsewhere.

Institution An "institution" includes private pension funds; mutual funds; public pension funds; foreign investors and institutions; life insurance companies; bank personal trusts; other insurance companies such as fire, casualty, and auto insurance; closed-end funds; broker/dealers; savings institutions; and commercial banks, according to the Federal Reserve.

In the early days, the people buying and selling shares of stocks were typically speculators and the very wealthy. By 1886, when the first one million shares were traded on the New York Stock Exchange, investing in equities had gone from an activity limited to an elite few to one in which nearly everyone could participate. But, from the stock market crash of 1929 up to the 1950s, investment professionals considered stocks to be too risky for the average individual.

In 1965, households—by a large margin—and not institutions owned most of the shares of stocks in the marketplace. That trend, however, is changing.

The following chart shows that in 1965, nearly 84 percent of the total market value of stocks was owned by households and a mere 16 percent held by institutions. But since that year, household ownership of equities has fallen and ownership by institutions risen. In 1985, 51 percent of stocks was owned by institutions, 49 percent by households. At year-end 1995 that split was reversed; approximately 51 percent of stocks was owned by individuals and 49 percent by households.

The Federal Reserve classifies those who own shares of stocks into two categories: households and institutions. Based on figures from the Federal Reserve Flow of Funds, here's a historic look at who owns U.S. equities.

YEAR	TOTAL MARKET $ VALUE	HOUSEHOLDS % OF MKT VALUE	INSTITUTIONS % OF MKT VALUE
1965	$735 billion	83.8 %	16.2 %
1970	841	68.0	32.0
1975	800	56.7	43.3
1980	1,535	60.2	39.8
1985	2,360	48.9	51.1
1990	3,530	49.9	50.1
1995	8,345	51.4	48.6

(Source: 1996 SIA Fact Book, p.56—their source, Federal Reserve Flow of Funds Accounts (revised))

ABOUT THE INDIVIDUAL SHAREHOLDER

While shareholders can be found in all walks of life and throughout all aspects of the business world, a New York Stock Exchange 1995 Shareownership Study shows that the average age of a shareholder is 45, has a median family income of $52,000 a year and a median portfolio of securities valued at $14,000.

The average stock shareholder is also likely to be working (76.5% are employed); has completed college (45.1%); and is married (79.4%).

Surprisingly, only 37.5 percent of them have a brokerage account and while they may own an IRA or Keogh (29.8%), or mutual fund (23.7%), over 42 percent own only one stock. And, a whopping 75 percent say that they are not willing to take risk.

Risk Don't think for one minute that investing in stocks is not risky business. Every investment you make has an element of risk to it. There are no risk-free investments in the stock market.

Two Things to Keep in Mind:

1. Not all stocks make their shareholders money.

2. Timing—as in when you sell and when you purchase your securities—is everything.

Here's a historic look at what percentage of the population owns shares of stock:

YEAR	NUMBER OF SHAREHOLDERS	U.S. POPULATION	PERCENT OF POPULATION
1952	6,490,000	156,216,000	4.2%
1962	17,010,000	185,206,000	9.2%
1970	30,850,000	204,766,000	15.1%
1983	42,360,000	229,178,000	18.5%
1990	51,440,000	243,680,000	21.1%

(Source: NYSE Shareownership surveys, as presented in 1996 Securities Industry Handbook, p. 57)

ABOUT THE INSTITUTIONS

The institutions that own stock include everything from private and public pension funds to mutual funds; life insurance companies; fire, casualty, and automobile insurance companies; foreign investors; and commercial banks.

With more and more individuals investing in stocks via mutual funds through employers' 401(k) plans, or for their own personal accounts and IRAs, it's easy to see how the category of "institutions" could wind up representing the largest holdings of stocks in the years to come.

In this lesson, you learned about who owns stocks. In the next lesson, you will learn why people—and institutions—own equities.

3

WHY PEOPLE BUY STOCKS

In this lesson, you will learn why people invest in stocks, what rights and privileges come with owning shares of stocks, and what kind of returns stocks have provided in the past.

WHY BUY STOCKS?

It's no mystery: Money is the primary reason stocks are bought—and eventually sold. Most people invest in stocks to make money from those investments, and the public corporations that issue stock do so to raise money.

Every year, nearly 3,000 companies trade more than 150 billion shares of stock worth more than $5 trillion dollars— and that's on the New York Stock Exchange alone!

Stock and bond markets, known as the *capital markets* to financial professionals, have been one of the primary sources of money for U.S. businesses throughout the years. Each year, hundreds of small businesses go to Wall Street to finance their growing businesses or to ensure they have money for research and development. Midsize and large companies often issue more shares of their company's stocks to finance the expansions of their companies as well. In fact, according to the

Securities Industry Association (the trade association for the securities industry), over $1.1 trillion was raised for business from the U.S. capital markets in 1995. With this money, jobs are created, new products are introduced, technology is advanced, and the general welfare of the economy can soar.

 Shareholder   One who owns shares in a corporation. People can be shareholders in corporations that are publicly owned, like those that trade on Wall Street; privately held, in which case shares are not publicly exchanged in the marketplace; or shareholders of investments companies—the technical term for mutual funds.

SHAREHOLDER RIGHTS AND PRIVILEGES

Knowing that money is the big deal behind every stock issued or purchased, being a shareholder in a company means you are an owner of that firm. As an owner you have certain rights and privileges, including...

- **A stock certificate, if you wish to have one.** In the old days, shareholders typically took physical possession of the shares of company stock they owned in the form of receiving that company's stock certificates. A stock certificate is a piece of paper (usually quite ornately adorned) that states—among other things—the name of the corporation, the number of shares you own, a *cusip number* that identifies the security issue, and the name of the owner of the shares.

But in today's fast-moving electronic world, in which computer entry is rapidly replacing paper, the issuance of stock certificates isn't as popular as it once was. So, instead of shareholders keeping their stock shares at home, in bank vaults, or safety deposit boxes, many stock certificates aren't sent to shareholders; the record of their stock ownership is electronically transferred to an individual's brokerage firm account.

- **The right to sell your shares, buy more of them, or transfer ownership of them to someone else.** That someone else could be a person or an institution, such as a charity.

- **The right to a dividend if the company decides to pay one.** There is no law stating that all publicly traded companies must pay dividends to their shareholders. Dividends, in fact, are like shareholder "perks," and not all companies pay them. A company's decision of when, if, and how much dividend to pay depends on two things: If they made a profit and have money to spend, and if they want to spend that money paying their shareholders a dividend. A company's board of directors decides whether or not to pay a dividend and how much it will be.

On Dividends   Dividends aren't guaranteed. Just because a company pays a dividend once is no guarantee that it will continue to pay dividends, or that future dividends will be equal to previous ones.

- **The right to your share in the growth—or demise—of a company.** As an owner in a publicly traded corporation, you get to share in that company's ups and downs. On the one hand, you'll enjoy the financial rewards of that company should the per-share value of that corporation's stock increase in value while you own shares of it. On the other, you'll share in the losses that company may go through if the value of its stock decreases.

When Companies Head South   What happens to shareholders when a company goes broke, closes its doors, and leaves oodles of debt behind? As a shareholder, the *worst* that can happen to you is the value of the shares you own will fall from the price you paid down to $0.00. Being a shareholder isn't like being a parent or someone's primary caregiver: The debts a company leaves behind are not your responsibility.

- **The right to be informed.** Shareholders are entitled to receive all sorts of information about the company they are part owner of. They are entitled to receive everything from the company's annual report to its corporate minutes to invitations to its annual meetings. Some companies even send samples of their products or discount coupons to their shareholders.

- **Voting rights.** With each share of stock you own comes one vote, provided the stock you own is not non-voting stock. In that case, voting privileges are waived.

Shareholders vote on things like whether or not they want the company sold, should a suitor be at hand, or for a change in the company's board of directors. Voting can be done in person—at a company's annual meeting, for instance. But for most shareholders, it's done by *proxy*, via the mail.

How much does your vote count? That depends upon how big a shareholder you are. If you own one share of XYZ corporation's 500,000 shares, your voting voice isn't very loud. On the other hand, if you're one of three shareholders who together own 75.9 percent of all stock issued by, say, American Media, Inc., publishers of the *National Enquirer* and other tabloids, you've got a big say in the way that company is run.

PERFORMANCE

Making money from stock investments is the name of the game. And while that's the goal, not all companies make money. Which means not all stocks make money for their shareholders all of the time.

Case in point: In May of 1996, a friend and I pretended we each had one million dollars to invest and set out to create our own portfolio of stocks. Without going into all the details, here's a look at the short-term performance of some of the stocks. Notice that all prices didn't go up.

NAME OF CO.	5/23/96 PRICE INITIAL DAY OF PURCHASE	6/6/96 PRICE	8/11/96 PRICE
Motorola	64 ⅞	64 ⅛	56 ¼
Schwab	24 ⅞	24 ¾	25 ⅜
Wrigley	52 ¾	53 ⅜	53 ½
Intel	70 ⅞	75 ¼	82 ⅜
United Healthcare Corp.	52 ⅞	55	39 ⅝

Looking back, stocks have earned an average of between 9 and 12 percent per year from 1926 through 1995, outperforming bonds by a large margin.

Stocks had their best performance during the 1950s when inflation was low and the business cycle high. During that decade, the Dow Jones Industrial Average rose 239.5 percent, or on average nearly 24 percent per year. The next best performing decade was the 1980s, when the Dow gained 228.3 percent—or an average of about 23 percent per year.

On the flip-side, the worst decade for stocks was the 1930s, when the DJIA actually declined 39.5 percent. That's an average loss of about 4 percent per year. The next worst per-forming decade for stocks was the 1970s. During that 10-year period the Dow gained a mere 4.8 percent, giving new meaning to the term *flat market*.

Flat Market   A *flat market* is when prices on stocks don't rally significantly as they did during the bull markets of the 1950s and 1980s or fall dramatically as they did during the bear market of the 1930s, but remain relatively stagnant—flat—as they did during the 1970s.

Crashes and Recoveries   Between 1929 and 1932, stock prices lost between 85-90 percent of their pre-crash values. The Dow Jones Industrial Average (DJIA), which peaked at 381.17 in September 1929, fell almost 90 percent to 41.22 on July 8, 1932. It took 25 years—until 1954— for the DJIA to surpass the high it attained in 1929.

On the other hand, every time the stock market has crashed, the DJIA has recovered. And not merely recovered to its old highs but to new ones.

One example of the fall and subsequent rise of a stock price after a crash is IBM, or "Big Blue" as the company's nicknamed. In October 1987, IBM hit a high of 174 ³/₄. But thanks to that year's stock market crash, by year's end the per-share price of that stock had dropped to $104; five years later, in 1993, it was trading in the $40-per-share range. Since then, Big Blue's been on the rise: On August 14, 1996, IBM finished trading at a per-share price of $111 ¹/₄.

Why buy stocks?   When it comes to the bottom line, there are two good reasons to buy stocks: One, in the hope that the per-share value of a stock will increase. This is referred to on Wall Street as *capital appreciation*. And two, for the dividend income a company may pay.

In this lesson, you learned why people invest in stocks and how stocks have performed. In the next lesson, you will learn about the various stock markets in the U.S.

4

THE STOCK MARKETS

In this lesson, you will learn about where the first stocks were traded, the various markets in which stocks are bought and sold, and who regulates the markets.

IN THE BEGINNING

Philadelphia, in 1790, was the home of the first U.S. stock market. But the streets of New York City are where the markets really gained their foothold.

Under a buttonwood tree on Wall Street is where traders in New York City met every day to exchange shares of stock, and where the notion of the New York Stock Exchange first found its roots. The year was 1792. In 1842, the New York Curb Exchange—so named because traders used to literally meet on the curb of the street—was created. In 1953, its name was changed to the American Stock Exchange.

These two exchanges are not the only stock exchanges in the country, but they are the two that have formed the cornerstone of the U.S. securities markets.

HOW STOCKS ARE TRADED

Stocks, as most of you know, are traded on markets, and a "market" is just another way of referring to the system used to trade securities like stocks.

If you look at the markets from the big picture, there are basically four types of markets: the *exchange market*, the *over-the-counter* (or *OTC*) *market*, and the third and fourth markets. It's on the first two, the exchange and the OTC, that individual investors do their trading.

Here's an overview of each:

- **The exchange market** This is the one we hear most about. It's made up of the two national exchanges, the New York Stock Exchange (NYSE) and the American Stock Exchange (AMEX)—both are private associations—and regional stock exchanges.

  To trade stocks on an exchange, one must first be a member of it, and then follow its rules and regulations. Members of an exchange are said to hold "seats" on the exchange. These seats, which on the NYSE can sell for anywhere from a few hundred thousand to millions of dollars depending upon market conditions, give a person or institution the opportunity to buy and sell listed securities on that exchange.

 Listed and Unlisted Securities A listed security is a stock, or bond, that's been accepted for trading on an exchange, like the NYSE or the AMEX. To be listed a company has to meet certain requirements set forth by the exchange. Unlisted securities are those that trade on NASDAQ and in the over-the-counter market.

- **The over-the-counter, or OTC market**   You'll find thousands upon thousands more stocks for sale on the OTC market than you will on all the exchange markets combined. That's because the OTC market is made up primarily of small and brand-new companies. The largest OTC market for stocks is NASDAQ.

  Unlike the exchanges, where the buying and selling of stocks occurs at one central place, there is no "home office" for the OTC market. Business for OTC stocks is conducted on the telephone and through a computerized quotation system.

Marked Differences   The difference between the exchange markets and the OTC market is how stock prices are arrived at.

The exchange markets, like the New York Stock Exchange, are *auction markets*: Supply and demand creates a security's price—stocks are sold to the highest bidder and bought for the lowest offer.

The OTC market is a *negotiated market*: Prices are worked out between buyer and seller. OTC security prices can vary from market-maker to market-maker. A *market-maker*, as the name implies, is a firm that owns a substantial amount of a stock that it sells through the OTC market.

- **The third market**   Created in the 1950s, this market is primarily for non-exchange member firms.

- **The fourth market**   This market is for the institutions and the direct trading among them. This market has been around since 1969 and allows buyers and sellers—such as equity traders, mutual funds, market-makers, and others—to negotiate trades anonymously among one another.

One quick way to differentiate stocks on the national exchanges from those in the over-the-counter markets is the number of letters in a stock symbol. Generally, stocks on the national exchanges use only one to three letters in a symbol; those on the OTC markets have four or five. The symbol for Ford is "F" and "CAT" is the symbol for Caterpillar; both companies trade on the national exchanges. The symbol for Apple Computers is "AAPL" and "CHKR" is Checkers Drive-In Restaurant, both trade on NASDAQ.

While we're on the subject of company names and their stock symbols, when you research or track a stock's performance in the newspaper, don't expect to find the same company stock symbol in your newspaper's listings. Newspapers use abbreviated names; stock symbols are not abbreviations—they're symbols. So, as an investor you've got three things to remember about a company name:

1. Its exact name.

2. The symbol for the class of share you purchased or are interested in.

3. The abbreviation used to identify it in the newspapers.

WHERE STOCKS ARE TRADED

Now that you know about the various kinds of markets and that trading stocks is done on the national exchanges, regional exchanges, and in the OTC marketplace, following is a listing of the names and addresses of the most popular U.S. stock exchanges:

THE NATIONAL STOCK EXCHANGES

- The New York Stock Exchange (NYSE). The NYSE, sometimes called "The Big Board" or "The Exchange," is the largest and best-known stock exchange in the country. Stocks listed on it are those of the largest and oldest companies around. As of the end of July 1996, there were nearly 2,800 stocks listed on this exchange and 3,400 issues traded. Some of them include General Electric, Motorola, and Disney.

  New York Stock Exchange (NYSE)
  11 Wall Street
  New York, NY 10005
  212-656-3000

- The American Stock Exchange (AMEX). Formed in 1842 as the New York Curb Exchange, many still refer to this exchange as the "Curb."

  Like the NYSE, trading on AMEX is auction style, based on supply and demand. There are approximately 465 members who trade on the AMEX, with nearly 800 companies listed and 910 different issues traded. Unlike the NYSE, companies listed here are smaller, newer ones with smaller trading volume than the larger company stocks listed on the NYSE. Two AMEX-listed stocks are Greyhound and HearX Ltd.

  The American Stock Exchange (AMEX)
  86 Trinity Place
  New York, NY 10006
  212-306-1000

Listed and Traded Issues   There's a difference between the number of *listed issues* and the number of *traded issues* on the two national exchanges, because a listed company may issue more than one class of stock. Consequently, the number of traded issues will be higher because it includes all classes of shares.

The number of issues traded for stocks on the regional exchanges is much higher than the number of stocks listed on each regional exchange because stocks may trade on more than one exchange.

REGIONAL STOCK EXCHANGES

Regional stock exchanges were originally developed to trade the stocks of local companies. Like the two national exchanges, the regional exchanges are auctions markets. Listing requirements for companies on these exchanges, however, aren't as tough as for those listed on the NYSE or AMEX. Many stocks listed on the national exchanges are also listed on the regional ones.

Some regional exchanges trade in stocks only, like the Cincinnati and the Boston Stock Exchanges. Others, like the Pacific and Philadelphia exchanges trade stocks, options, warrants, and rights.

Here's a list of the largest regional exchanges along with the number of stocks listed on them as of mid-August 1996.

- **Boston Stock Exchange, Inc. (BE)**
  One Boston Place, 38th Floor
  Boston, MA 02108
  617-723-9500

175 companies listed on this exchange
2,300 issues traded

- **The Chicago Stock Exchange (CHX)**
  (Formerly called the Midwest Exchange)
  440 South LaSalle
  Chicago, IL 60605
  312-663-2222

  250 companies listed here
  3,700 issues traded

- **The Chicago Board Options Exchange (CBOE)**
  LaSalle at Van Buren
  Chicago, IL 60605
  312-786-5600

  600 stocks are listed here, as well as stock options.

- **Philadelphia Stock Exchange (PHLX)**
  1900 Market Street
  Philadelphia, PA 19103
  215-496-5000

  70 companies listed here
  3,000 issues traded

- **Pacific Stock Exchange Incorporated (PSE)**
  233 South Beaudry Avenue, 12th Floor
  Los Angeles, CA 90012
  213-977-4500

  97 companies listed
  2,415 issues traded here

- **The Cincinnati Stock Exchange (CSE)**
  (Moved to Chicago)
  400 South LaSalle
  Chicago, IL 60605
  312-786-8803

510 stocks traded

0 sole listings

THE OVER-THE-COUNTER MARKET

The over-the-counter market got its name from buyers and sellers who quite literally bought and sold securities by passing their orders back and forth over the counter in a brokerage firm. Today, OTC stocks are traded over phone lines through a network of computers called the National Market System (NMS).

NASDAQ lists stocks in two separate categories:

- NASDAQ National Market, consisting of more than 3,500 of the larger, typically more actively traded companies

- NASDAQ SmallCap Market, consisting of more than 1,300 smaller growth companies

Very small companies—like the tiny ones whose stocks often trade for pennies, or fractions of them per share—that trade in the OTC market and aren't a part of NASDAQ, can be found in what's called the *pink sheets*. This listing of stocks is actually printed on pink paper and is published every day.

OTC and NASDAQ Sometimes the terms OTC and NASDAQ may seem interchangeable—one referring to the other and vise versa. In reality, OTC stands for the "over-the-counter" market, whereas NASDAQ is the acronym for the National Association of Securities Dealers Automated Quotation system, a computerized system that provides stock prices, or stock "quotes," to stock brokers and dealers for the stocks traded in the OTC market.

WHO REGULATES THE MARKETS?

Some of the very good things that came out of the stock market crash of 1929 were the creations of new U.S. securities laws. These laws have made the securities industry in our country one of the most regulated in the world, which in turn plays a large part in the success our securities industry enjoys.

Keeping an eye out for who's minding the stock store is done on a variety of levels including the federal and state levels, exchange and other self-regulatory levels, as well as on the personal and individual level.

The primary watchdog of the securities industry on the federal level is the Securities and Exchange Commission (SEC). The SEC exists because of two acts passed after the Crash of 1929: The Securities Act of 1933 and the Securities Exchange Act of 1934.

The first, the Securities Act of 1933, was originally called the Truth in Securities Act. And, as that name implies, prior to it, truth and trading securities may not have always gone hand-in-hand. This act, among other things, required that any security, before it is offered for sale to the public, must first be registered and that disclosure about a company's financial picture be made available to interested investors.

It was the Securities Exchange Act of 1934 that actually allowed for the creation of the SEC and for that federal agency to administer what was laid out in the Securities Act of 1933. This act is sometimes referred to as the Exchange Act. Some of the issues covered in it include outlawing any misrepresentations and/or manipulations of securities, the registration of broker/dealers, and regulation of insider transactions, trading activities, client accounts, and the OTC market.

The National Association of Securities Dealers (NASD) was created in 1939 to oversee the OTC market and NASDAQ. And, mutual-fund investors will be pleased to know that the law regulating their investments is the Investment Company Act of 1940. An "investment company" is another way of saying "mutual fund."

All of the exchanges have self-regulatory aspects, meaning that each has its own set of rules and regulations. And on the state level, there are *blue sky* laws that require the sellers of new stock issues and mutual funds to be registered within the states where they intend to solicit business.

From an independent point of view, firms selling securities have their own set of business ethics and standards for their employees and sales people. Sales individuals also have their own set of business ethics they subscribe to. And along with all these layers of regulatory bodies, including those not mentioned, is the media and press. Not a weekday goes by without a host of TV, radio, and newspapers reporting about what's happened on Wall Street. Regulating the securities industry, therefore, is something we Americans watch very closely.

"Hello, SEC?"   If you'd ever like to get in touch with the Securities & Exchange Commission, to register a complaint or a compliment, write to

The Office of Consumer Affairs
Securities and Exchange Commission
450 5th Street N.W.
Washington, D.C. 20549

In this lesson, you learned about the various U.S. stock markets and who regulates them. In the next lesson, you will learn about the different kinds of stock that are traded in those marketplaces.

THE DIFFERENT KINDS OF STOCK

In this lesson, you will learn about the different kinds of stock that companies issue.

THE SKINNY ON STOCKS

Just as there are a number of different uses for the word "stock"—among other things it can refer to a company's inventory or even cattle—there are a number of different kinds of stocks that companies can issue. Each one appeals to the different needs investors have—preferred stocks, for instance, provide income for shareholders, and penny stocks satisfy the "Who knows? This stock could make me millions!" desire of others. And, each has its benefits and own shareholder rights.

As you learned in earlier lessons, stocks are issued by corporations to raise money from the investing public—trade on various stock exchanges and when you purchase even one share of a corporate stock, you're an owner in that company.

Basically, there are two different types of stock—common stock and preferred. There's also an alphabet of different share classes beginning with A, B, C, and so on, that may be issued.

Unfortunately, there are no carved-in-granite rules regarding what each class of stock represents. So, one company's B shares may have rights, while another company's won't. That means once the definitions of common and preferred stock are understood, the characteristics of each class will differ from company to company, as will the risk and potential rewards, dividend payments, price appreciation, and shareholder rights. It is therefore up to you, the investor, to find out all about the class of stock you've invested in and what rights and privileges go along with it.

COMMON STOCKS

Common stocks are the most popular kind of stock issued and consequently are owned by more people and institutions than any other kind of stock.

When you buy shares of a common stock, you're part owner of the company issuing the stock and will share in the risks and rewards of that company. Plus, you will be entitled to receive any dividends the company declares—if the company decides to pay them. Dividends are either paid in the form of cash or as a *stock dividend*—which means instead of being paid money you would acquire more shares of that company's stock. But, no matter whether the company does or does not pay a dividend, if that company's stock price rises, the value of your shares will also increase. Yahoo!

 Counting on Dividends   Remember, as you learned in Lesson 3, the price of a stock and the frequency of dividend payments may fluctuate. Depending on market conditions and how much money a company makes, a company may or may not decide to pay a dividend at certain times.

Similarly, if a company has fallen on hard times or is out of favor with the investing public, the shares you own may decrease in value, no matter what's going on with that company's dividend policy.

Owning shares of common stock more often than not means you'll have *voting rights* in that company. Voting rights give you a say in corporate policies and management decisions. Since it's not always possible to attend a company's annual shareholder meeting where voting is typically done, the bulk of today's shareholders vote on corporate concerns by *proxy*, which allows you to be a part of the voting process when you can't be there in person.

Proxy voting works like this: A company mails a proxy statement and proxy voting card to each shareholder prior to the shareholder meeting. The statement explains the issues to be voted on—like a change in the board of directors—and the proxy card is like a ballot. Shareholders register their votes on the proxy card and then mail it back to the company. The weight your vote carries depends upon what percentage of the company shares you own.

Classified Stock and Founders Shares
Companies may issue more than one class of common stock, such as Class A and Class B shares, and so on. The stock classes don't just stop with "B" but can go up depending upon the corporate financing needs of the company. These classes of stock are called *classified stock*, and each one has its own investment parameters. If you invest in a company's classified shares, make sure you understand the rights and privileges of

each. You can find this information from your broker or better yet, from the company's shareholder services department.

Founders stock is another kind of common stock. These shares, too, have their own rewards, including voting rights for the company's founders.

COMMON STOCKS AND ECONOMIC ENVIRONMENTS

Looking at the universe of common stocks from another point of view, stocks are sometimes lumped into different groupings depending upon their dividend payment history, what the company makes, what they hope to make and what's happening in the economy.

For instance, *income producing stocks* refer to a company that has had a long history of consistently paying dividends. *Blue chip stocks* represent those offered by the largest and best-established companies in America, and *emerging growth stocks* refer to new companies' stocks.

There are also *defensive* or *staple stocks,* like those from food and pharmaceutical companies, so called because their market values aren't supposed to get hurt as badly as other groupings of stocks when there is a downturn in the economy or when the country is in a recession. The performance of *cyclical stocks,* like those that produce durable goods such as paper, cement, and steel, usually depends upon business cycles; when there's a flurry of new homes being built across the country, companies manufacturing concrete and steel are likely to prosper.

Penny stocks are those whose per share prices are less than $1. These are considered very risky investments, and there's no telling how an investment in them will fare no matter what the economic environment is.

There is more about stock types and their "personalities" in Lesson 7.

PREFERRED STOCK

Like common stock, preferred stock represents ownership in a company, but with a few added perks. First of all, preferred stocks pay dividends, and those dividends get paid to preferred shareholders before any dividends are paid to shareholders of a company's common stock.

Another perk for the preferred stock shareholder is, if a company should belly-up (go bankrupt), after all creditors are paid, holders of preferred stock have a claim to the remaining assets of the corporation— if there are any. Their claim to those assets gets first dibs—ahead of shareholders of the company's common stock.

On the other hand, the shareholders of preferred stocks often don't have voting rights. Plus, these stocks don't usually have the growth potential that common stocks do. That's why preferred stocks are considered similar to bonds: Both are without voting privileges, the size of the dividend to be paid is usually fixed, and price appreciation isn't the primary reason for buying the security—income is.

Like common stocks, there's not just one kind of preferred stock that can be issued. Some of the more popular kinds of preferred stocks are:

- **Cumulative preferred** Shareholders of this kind of preferred stock know that if the company misses any dividend payments, they have the right to receive all of what's owed to them sometime in the future when the company resumes its dividend payment schedule.

- **Participating preferred**   Along with dividend income, and after all dividends have been paid, shareholders of this kind of preferred stock can participate in the dividend increases.

- **Adjustable rate preferred**   Dividends on this stock will fluctuate according to changes in interest rates.

- **Convertible preferred**   Shares here can be converted into a specified number of common stock shares at a date sometime in the future.

- **Callable preferred**   These shares can be "called" back to the company at a future date. That means the company has the right to buy back the stock from its shareholders at pre-stated per-share prices.

STOCK WARRANTS AND STOCK RIGHTS

In addition to common and preferred stocks, companies may also issue stock warrants and stock rights. Both are similar in that they allow investors the right to buy stock at a future date at a specific price.

Stock rights are a short-term proposition that work like this: If a company that already is publicly traded decides to issue some new shares of stock, stock rights may be issued to give existing company shareholders the opportunity to buy some of those new issue shares below the current market price on the date the stock is to be issued. The amount of stock a shareholder may purchase in a stock rights offering will be in proportion to the number of shares already owned.

Stock warrants are longer-term deals. Holders won't receive any dividends or retain other rights of stock ownership, but they do have the opportunity to purchase a specific number of shares of common stock at a later day, at a specified price.

Warrants may or may not trade on the exchanges like stocks do. Those that do provide a way for speculators, who expect the price of the stock to rise above the one set forth by the warrant, to play the market. But the main idea behind stock warrants is value-added incentives. Here's why: If a warrant allows you to buy a set number of shares of a stock below the current market price, doing so would give that warrant intrinsic value. That is, you could use the warrant to purchase the stock, then turn around and sell that stock and make a profit. Sweet deal when it happens.

Warrants often have expiration dates 5 and 10 years from their date of issuance. A warrant that comes attached with a new stock issue is called a *unit*.

In this lesson, you learned about the different kinds of stock issued by companies and what your rights as a shareholder are. In the next lesson, you will learn more about IPOs and where the money goes after a stock starts trading.

WHERE THE MONEY GOES

In this lesson, you will learn about initial public offerings and the primary and secondary markets in which stocks trade.

Understanding the various stocks and the markets in which they trade is one thing; knowing how stocks get to market and start the trading process is quite another.

To understand how that happens, and where the money traded in stocks day-in and day-out goes, it's best to think BIG.

For openers, while all corporations that are formed issue stock, not all stock is publicly traded. Your cousin Maybelle might own a bakery shop that is incorporated, but all shares may be divided among her, her best friend Beth, and her Uncle Willie. While the value of each share of stock is stated in corporate papers, the stock is privately owned. When it is exchanged, it's usually done among a closely knit group of people.

But a publicly owned corporation is an animal of a different color. These companies are generally quite large and employ a number of people. They also have made the management decision to go to the marketplace to pick up the cash necessary to see that their business stays competitive and hopefully continues to grow. This decision on Wall Street is referred to as "going public." And, the first time a brand-new company decides to go public, its stock offering is called an initial public offering, or IPO. IPOs trade on what is referred to as the *primary market.*

THE PRIMARY MARKET

There wouldn't be a stock market if there weren't a primary market. The primary market is where it all begins, how the money machine gets moving, and where established businesses and entrepreneurs raise the cash they need to get or keep their businesses rolling.

Two kinds of stock trade in the primary market—Initial Public Offerings, or IPOs, and new issue shares of already established, publicly owned companies.

Every publicly traded company gets its Wall Street feet wet as an IPO. In a nutshell, here's what it takes for a company to go public:

First, after making the decision to become a public company, knowing fair-well that decision means giving up some power, the company contacts an investment banker or brokerage firm to handle the "going public" process from beginning to end. That investment banker or brokerage firm then finds *underwriters* for the stock. One thing underwriters do is agree to purchase a specific number of stock and then sell it to the public.

Before the stock can be sold to the public, it has to be registered with the Securities and Exchange Commission (SEC). During this registration process, a specific number of shares that are to be traded is decided upon; the company's financial data must all be disclosed; potential investors need to be notified about the new stock offering through what's called a "tombstone ad" in the newspaper (it's called a tombstone ad because of the fine-line border around it, but more importantly, because it isn't an ad soliciting sales but one of notification); and finally, a *prospectus* is created and made available to prospective buyers.

 Prospectus A printed summary of a company's business outlook, including its current and future business plans, which describes the details of the company and of the current stock offering including risks. A prospectus is a legal document that must be given to every investor who purchases a registered security during its initial offering.

The moneys received from the sale of an IPO get placed in an *escrow account* until all the shares of that offering are sold. After they are sold, the offering is said to be "closed" and a transfer agent records, distributes, and releases share ownership accordingly.

One of the continuing roles of the underwriters of an IPO is to "make a market" in the company's shares after the initial offering date. So, the next time you see an ad in the business section of your newspaper announcing a stock offering, all the names listed in the bottom section of that announcement will be the names of that stock's underwriters.

Along with providing a company with cash, going public can help a company gain recognition—but the move also opens its financial books to scrutiny.

New issue stocks also trade on the primary market until all shares are sold. The difference between a new issue and an IPO is that new issues come from established companies that have decided to raise capital by issuing more stock, and from companies already trading on the exchanges. IPOs don't.

IPOs IPOs are hot properties these days. Since the early 1980s—when individuals got their share of the IPO market until today when the big institutions and mutual funds gobble up all shares first—these new stocks have, in some cases, made profits look easy to make.

According to two professors who studied the performance of the 4,753 IPOs that came to market between 1970 to 1990, the best performance results happen during an IPO stock's first day of trading. The study found that from the first through the fifth year of trading, the average annual returns on an IPO lagged other stocks by 7 percentage points. This led the professors to conclude that if investors don't get in on an IPO before trading begins, they are better off investing in established companies.

Marketing IPOs In an effort to gain more attention, companies bringing IPOs to market are doing more and more IPO marketing. Models are showing up on the exchanges, hawking the wares of everything from perfume companies to restaurants. Even cigars were passed around during the recent IPO of Consolidated Cigar. The good news regarding Consolidated Cigar is not only that the cigars were great, but the stock's price ended the day ahead of where it opened. (It opened at $23 and ended at $28 ⅜.)

But just because this IPO had a great first day doesn't mean they all will. Investors need to be aware that the marketing of IPOs is one thing and the performance of the underlying stock is quite another.

THE SECONDARY MARKETS

After a stock makes its debut and all shares of the IPO or new issue allocations are sold, it begins trading in the secondary markets. They're the ones most investors are familiar with.

Unlike money raised through an IPO or new issue, which, after fees are paid to investment bankers and others involved in the process, goes to the company itself, the money exchanged as stocks are bought and sold in the secondary markets goes to the seller of the stock. That means people like you or me. Or, the money goes to companies that own stocks in their portfolios like banks, insurance companies, and mutual funds. In other words, once a stock starts trading on the secondary markets, the money from the sale of that stock belongs to the people or institutions trading it and not the corporation that issued it.

WHAT AFFECTS A STOCK'S PRICE?

What a grand world it would be if there were a guarantee ensuring us that the stock we bought would always go up in value and make us money. Unfortunately, there are a zillion reasons why a stock's price may increase in value—and just as many reasons why it may not. Either of these may be substantiated by a company's financial picture; based on investors' sentiments, timing, and emotions; or reflect a combination of all of the above.

Most money managers have specific investing guidelines that they follow as they weed through the thousands of stocks available looking for the ones they hope will increase in value over the years. Some look for companies that have a price-earnings ratio of under 12. Some want companies that have no outstanding debt. Others want a company's sales to have grown by at least 20 percent for the last five years before they'd be interested buyers. Most want the company's stock to trade actively. Some want all of the above and some have other lists of criteria that they follow.

But no matter what financial fundamentals a money manager looks for before deciding whether or not to invest in a company, he or she knows that there is more to stock picking than the bottom line. Things like business cycles, natural disasters, and political and social events can all affect the prices on stocks as does the time of the year, and just plain timing in general.

Emotions can also play a part in how the market is reacting to certain stocks as can an optimistic—*bullish*—or pessimistic—*bearish*—economic outlook.

All of which means there's usually not just one reason why the price of a stock moves over the short- to medium-run. Over the long haul, however, prices—as reflected by the Dow Jones Industrial Average—have moved upward. Keep in mind that just because the Dow is moving upward doesn't mean the stock or stocks you've invested in have. The Dow Jones Industrial Average is an *average* of 30 stocks, and as such is merely a reflection of the blue chip market. Your portfolio of stocks is the another thing, and needs to be monitored as such.

In this lesson, you learned about IPOs and new issues, about the primary and secondary markets, and what can affect the price of stocks. In the next lesson you'll learn about the different stock personalities.

7

STOCK
PERSONALITIES

In this lesson, you will learn about the various groupings of stocks and the underlying characteristics of each.

As you learned in Lesson 5, stocks may be either common or preferred, and can also be grouped depending upon things like the size of company, industry, or performance style. All of which means there is no shortage of choices when it comes to types of stocks to pick from.

To keep things as simple as possible, when it comes to understanding the entire universe of stocks, think about them as having personalities. And often, the kind of stock you invest in depends upon your personality too—such as your investment objectives, if you're investing for income or for growth, and the risks you are willing to take.

Depending on who you talk to, any number of stock personalities can be found. But to keep things simple, this lesson describes seven of the most common, and some of the personality traits of each:

GROWTH STOCK

If anything whets the appetite of investors, it's the prospect that the per-share price of a stock is going to not just move ahead slowly but surely, but *soar*. Growth stocks hold that possibility because they typically represent new and expanding companies whose market values can appreciate quickly.

Depending on the company, growth stocks usually don't pay dividends since most of the company's profits get plowed back into it to further its growth and development. If they do pay dividends, they are often small. Growth stocks usually sell at high price-earnings multiples, probably don't have long-term well-established performance histories, and might be considered to be risky investments. But what makes them attractive investments isn't necessarily just their price-earnings multiples but how fast the earnings of the company are growing.

 Price-Earnings Ratio (P/E) If you're looking for a quick way to figure out how much you are paying for a company's stock in relationship to its earnings, look at its price-earnings multiple, or P/E ratio, as it's commonly referred to.

A P/E ratio is figured by dividing the price per share of a stock by its earnings per share. So, if XYZ Corporation's price per share is $20, and its earnings per share is $2, the P/E is 10 (20 divided by 2). Similarly, if ABC Company's price per share is $20, and its earnings per share $1, then its P/E would be 20.

A general rule of thumb is, the higher a stock's P/E, the riskier—or more aggressive—an investment it is. So, using the examples above, ABC would be considered a more aggressive investment based upon the company's P/E ratio.

UNDERVALUED STOCK

If you're a bargain hunter in the shopping world, you'll probably take a shine to undervalued stocks in the securities world.

Undervalued stocks, often called *value stocks*, have typically been overlooked by money managers and investors. They may have fallen out of favor with investors because of current trends in the market, but nonetheless may be stocks from secure, well-established companies with solid balance sheets.

One key to finding an undervalued stock is to look at past performance. If the stock of a well-established company has a history of performing well in the past (steadily increasing its dividend if it pays one), makes a good product that continues to sell, and has a solid financial picture, the stock could be a great buy for value-conscious investors. On the other hand, an undervalued stock could be undervalued for another reason— perhaps there are management problems and as a result the company has fallen on difficult times.

Unlike growth stocks that typically represent new companies, finding undervalued stocks to invest in can be a conservative way to invest in established companies that others have over-looked and that could perform handsomely in the future. Finding the value, however, begins with doing your home-work.

What's growth and what's value? The basic difference between growth and value investing, or investing in undervalued stocks, is *growth investors* believe that, if a company is selling its product and making more money year after year, no matter how the P/E reads, the price will *appreciate* (go up in value).

Value investors look almost solely at a company's price-earnings ratio. Buying stocks with low price-earnings ratios lowers the downside risk, unless the earnings of the company fall apart.

Just as there are differences between growth and value stocks, there are similarities too: Neither one comes with guaranteed with results.

BLUE CHIP STOCK

The big guys on Wall Street are the blue chip stocks. They make up the 30 stocks in the Dow Jones Industrial Average. They are the companies whose names we quickly recognize, like McDonald's, Coca-Cola, and Johnson & Johnson.

Blue chip stocks represent the stable, profitable, well-known companies that have a solid history of steady revenue growth and dividend payouts.

Investors who like the blue chips aren't looking for pizzazz. They're looking for quality. They're also looking for companies whose per-share prices may be relatively high, but stable— companies they can feel secure about, and whose price appreciation is likely to be steady no matter what market conditions are. Provided, of course, the company is still selling solid wares, staying out of court, and generally performing up to its blue chip name.

SMALL COMPANY STOCK

Small company stocks are just as their name implies: The stocks of companies whose market capitalization is small— usually less than $500 million up to $1 billion, depending on who's doing the defining. Here again, there is no one clear-cut, Wall Street definition of how much capital differentiates a small-cap company from a mid-cap one. What one person calls a small-cap company, another calls a mid-cap; it's important to remember small-cap stocks are more growth-oriented, and considered more aggressive investments than blue chip or other growth stocks. With any luck at all, however, small-cap stocks can grow into large-cap stocks and eventually blue chips. Microsoft is a great example of that.

So, while the performance of small-cap stocks is historically more volatile, this type of stock can also be more financially rewarding.

Market Capitalization   Market capitalization is a company's overall dollar worth, determined by multiplying the stock price by the number of shares outstanding. For instance, a stock with 5 million shares outstanding selling at $20 per share would have a market capitalization of $100 million (5 million × $20).

CYCLICAL STOCK

Housing, automobile, and paper stocks are examples of cyclical stocks. They are called cyclical because their earnings and stock prices have a tendency to rise when the economy is strong and fall when the economy is falling or in a recession.

Cyclical stock also refers to companies that make durable goods such as paper products or cars.

NONCYCLICAL STOCK

Tobacco, drug, and food companies are considered noncyclical because the demand for their products remains constant no matter what's happening to the market or the country's economy.

Noncyclical stocks are often large blue-chip companies, which is why many money pros considered them a staple when creating long-term stock portfolios; they have a tendency to be more cycle-proof than other stocks.

MULTINATIONAL STOCK

Investing outside of the U.S. is not only being talked about a lot but is becoming a very popular practice for some investors. In fact, the next lesson is about that very subject.

But, back to U.S. multinational stocks—if you're reluctant to invest outside of America but still like the idea of doing so, buying shares of a multinational company could be for you.

Multinational U.S. stocks basically represent our homegrown companies that also conduct business in countries outside of our borders. McDonald's, Pepsi, Toys 'R' Us, and Coca-Cola are all multinational companies, having stores and selling products all around the world. In fact, in 1995, well over half of Coke's revenues came from outside the U.S.

Owning shares of a well-established blue-chip multinational company is one way to diversify your portfolio in a creatively conservative fashion; owning shares of a small-cap company just beginning to do business overseas is a whole lot riskier.

Risk-Taking and Stock Personalities   They say people have to read something 13 times before it sinks in, so let me again write that there are *no guarantees* when it comes to the stock market, *and* investing in any stock means taking on some degree of risk.

Knowing that, the most anyone can lose when buying individual shares of stock is the money they invested and the commission costs surrounding the trade.

Stocks Grouped by Industry

Along with grouping stocks based on their personalities, stocks can also be broken down by industry. Then within any given industry, a company could fall into any of the seven personality types listed above.

Here are a few of the industry groupings for stocks. Again, these categories are broad-stroke ones, and, some of the subheads are considered to be industries of their own by some money managers:

- **Retail**, which typically includes men's and ladies' apparel, footwear, and jewelry

- **Gaming stocks**, including casinos

- **Lodging**

- **Computers**, including software companies

- **Telecommunications utilities**, including gas, electric, and telephone

- **Pharmaceuticals**

- **Financial**, including banks, savings and loans, and brokerage businesses

- **Real estate**

In this lesson, you learned about different stock personalities, risk, and the industries that stocks fall under. In the next lesson, you will learn about the international stock markets.

8

INTERNATIONAL STOCKS

In this lesson, you will learn about the international marketplace, what appeal it holds for stock investors, how to buy stocks abroad, and some of the risks of international investing.

Once upon a time, stocks on the U.S. exchanges accounted for the bulk of the market capitalization of all stocks traded around the world. Today, however, that's not so: Only about one-third of the world's market capitalization is made up of U.S. stocks. That leaves two-thirds to come from securities sold on other markets around the planet. That change in the size of the markets has people with money know-how talking about the benefits of investing outside of our own shores.

If you were sitting on the moon, able to see all the economic developments taking place on Earth, you'd see growth in countries all over the world. In China, for instance, the economy has grown at an average rate of around 10 percent per year for the past few years. Comparing that with the U.S., where our annual growth rate has hovered around 3 percent, you can see there's more growth going on in China. China, however, is not the only spot offering international investment opportunities. They exist almost everywhere, including South and Central America, Canada, Africa, Australia, Asia, and Europe.

But, just as the U.S. market may have looked to those living in London 150 or 200 years ago—a highly speculative and certainly risky bet—international investing doesn't appeal to everyone.

WHAT TO EXPECT

The reason anyone invests is to make money, whether those investments are in securities such as stocks, or in commodities, like grains or precious metals. The reason anyone invests outside the U.S. is also to make money. But to make money in foreign stocks on foreign stock markets takes extra skill.

In the securities world, there is no stock market as precise or regulated as the one in the United States. Most countries don't have a Securities and Exchange Commission. Some countries don't even have one centralized place to trade securities, and stocks are often traded in sections of stores or on the streets as securities once were here. Nor are accounting systems centralized all over the globe. Neither is the value of money. Or executive points of view. Or business ethics, employee work conditions, or product-quality controls. All of which means that there can be far more risk to investing in a company based outside the U.S. than in one here at home.

On the other hand, who hasn't heard of companies like the food maker Nestlé, the Swiss pharmaceutical Roche, or Ericson telephones? All three are international companies whose products are well-respected and whose companies many consider blue chips.

In 1995, Americans bought $51.2 billion in foreign equities, according to the Securities Industry Association. That's over five times more than $9.2 billion in 1990, and over 14 times the $3.8 billion purchased in 1985.

So, while it's safe to say that international investing is becoming more and more popular and the global investing world is getting smaller and smaller, that doesn't mean all markets perform in tandem with one another.

In 1995, for instance, when the U.S. market roared ahead over 37 percent, stocks in the United Kingdom (UK.) gained roughly 23 percent, and in Italy and Japan stocks actually lost money, as the following chart shows:

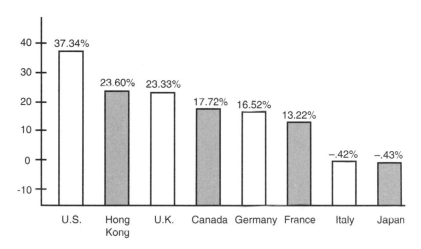

Figure 8.1   1995 Equity Market Returns (in U.S. Dollar Terms)

After looking at that graph, the obvious question is, if the U.S. is outperforming so many other markets in the world, why bother to invest outside? The answer is simple: Because year-in and year-out, the U.S. markets don't outperform other markets. In fact, according to Merrill Lynch, the top performing markets in the world during this decade have been:

1990	Mexico	+37%
1991	Brazil	+295%
1992	Peru	+123%

1993	Turkey	+197%
1994	Brazil	+60%
1995	Switzerland	+38%

So, for anyone who sees the world as full of investing opportunities and wants to create a diversified stock portfolio, investing abroad makes logical sense.

HOW TO INVEST INTERNATIONALLY

There are four popular ways to invest in the securities of other countries. The first is to buy shares of a stock that are listed and trade on the U.S. markets, like Grand Metropolitan, the U.K. company that owns Burger King, or Philippine Long Distance, or Benetton, the Italian clothier.

Another way is to purchase ADRs—American Depository Receipts, or receipts for shares of foreign companies. Owning them gives stockholders the right to receive any company dividends, they just don't receive the stock certificates themselves. There are thousands of ADRs on the market, one of which is Coles Myer Ltd., the largest retailer in Australia.

A third way to invest internationally, as mentioned in Lesson 7, is to purchase shares of U.S. multinational companies, like Exxon, Gillette, or hundreds of other corporations that have a business presence in other parts of the world.

And the fourth is to invest in global and/or international mutual funds. There are nearly 900 different global and international stock funds for investors to choose from within the mutual fund arena. Some invest in specific regions of the world, like Latin America or Japan; others invest internationally in small-cap funds; still others in the stocks traded on the emerging markets. There is more about mutual fund investing in Lesson 18.

In the end, retail stock brokers are trading more and more foreign stocks for individual U.S. investors every day. In 1996, Merrill Lynch reported that it now trades about 4,000 foreign stocks for its retail clients—that's up substantially from the 600 stocks it traded two years earlier. By the year 2000, who knows? The world may have one centralized stock market that everyone can easily tap into and use.

RISKS OF INTERNATIONAL INVESTING

There are five main risk factors every investor has to consider before investing abroad:

Political
Social
Economic
Language
Currency

Mexico is a prime example of a country that offers investors a world of investing opportunity and at the same time illustrates the risks of international investing.

In the early 1990s, Mexico was enjoying an economic rebound, with inflation under control, stocks doing well (the Mexican market was the world's hottest performer in 1990), and a government whose president was widely respected. Then, in what seemed an instant, what is now referred to as the "Tequila Effect" happened, turning all that was economically rosy in Mexico upside-down. Stock prices tumbled, government officials changed, inflation picked up, and the value of the peso—which had stabilized—jumped all over.

Political changes, social unrest, changes in a country's currency values, and natural disasters can all damage a country's stock market performance. Language can also be a problem for the international investor, particularly if they can't speak, read, or write in the language of the country whose companies they want to invest in.

So there's plenty to worry about if you're conservative by nature and are considering investing outside the United States. Then again, even the most conservative investor can't completely overlook the numerous investment opportunities that exist around the world. That's why many investors who want to own stocks of international companies but don't feel they have the expertise to pick those stocks have opted for investing in global and international mutual funds. That way they can let the portfolio manager of the fund do the stock picking.

The world is literally a marketplace for stocks. Following is a table showing the global stock markets and the emerging markets of the world. Both are from Barron's.

GLOBAL STOCK MARKETS	EMERGING MARKETS
Australia	Argentina
Austria	Brazil
Belgium	Chile
Canada	China Free
Denmark	Colombia
Finland	Czech Republic
France	Greece
Germany	Hungary

Hong Kong	India
Ireland	Indonesia
Italy	Israel
Japan	Jordan
Malaysia	Korea
Netherlands	Mexico
New Zealand	Pakistan
Norway	Peru
Singapore	Philippines
Spain	Poland
Sweden	Portugal
Switzerland	So. Africa
United Kingdom	Sri Lanka
U.S.A.	Taiwan
	Thailand
	Turkey
	Venezuela

In this lesson, you learned about the international stock markets and the risks involved when investing in them. In the next lesson, you will learn about dividend-paying stocks.

9

DIVIDEND PAYING STOCKS

In this lesson, you will learn about stocks that pay dividends.

It wasn't long ago that brokers referred to some stocks as being good for "widows and orphans." Those stocks were usually from well-established companies that had a solid track record of price stability and of paying dividends. Blue chip stocks like Kellogg's and utility stocks like Northern States Power fell into that category.

Dividends, as mentioned earlier, are paid out of a company's earnings. To pay them, the company first has to have the money. After that, it's up to the company's board of directors to decide if, when, and how much dividend is to be paid. More often than not, dividends are paid in cash—although they may be paid in the form of additional stock. And, they are usually paid on a quarterly basis, or once every three months.

THE DIVIDEND ENVIRONMENT ON WALL STREET

Dividend yields have been falling for the past 10 years on Wall Street. In mid-1986, the average yield on dividend-paying stocks on the S & P 500 was about 3.3 percent. Today's dividend yield averages about 2.3 percent—one full percentage point lower. One reason for the lower dividend yields revolves around the way today's corporate executives are managing their businesses.

Years ago, maintaining—if not increasing—a company's dividend was very much in vogue. That strategy was one way a company could tell its shareholders that it was prospering and doing well. Today, management doesn't necessarily talk that same language. Instead, many firms have decided to buy back shares of their company's outstanding stock rather than pay a dividend or increase what they are paying.

While stock buybacks often result in the per share price of the stock rising, it doesn't allow for any cash flow to shareholders—unless, of course, the shareholders sell some of the shares they own, or they own shares of the company's preferred stock. In which case the dividends must be paid.

Where to Get Cash   If you absolutely positively need income, consider purchasing a company's preferred rather than common stock. The big advantage is that a company must pay dividends to its preferred shareholders before it pays its common stock shareholders.

Another plus is that the dividend on preferred stocks won't fluctuate as on common stock, because the dividend is fixed and investors know how much their preferred stock investment will pay them. On the other hand, don't look for dividend increases on preferred stock.

TAXES AND DIVIDENDS

As mentioned earlier, companies typically pay their dividends in the form of cash or stock. If a company pays its dividends in stock, depending upon the number of shares you own, the dividend may come in full or fractional shares. Don't be concerned about those fractional shares; over time, fractional shares add up to full ones and will increase the total number of shares you own in the company.

Another benefit to receiving a company's dividend payment in the form of stock rather than cash is taxes. Stock dividends aren't taxed when you receive them. The only time you'll ever pay taxes on any shares of stock you own—dividend-paying or otherwise—is when you sell those shares at a higher price than what your cost basis on that stock is. (A *cost basis* is the per-share price paid for a security that includes commission costs.) That means you control when a *capital gains tax*—which you pay when you sell your stock for more than you paid for it—is paid.

When a company pays its dividends in cash, however, you have to pay taxes on those cash dividends in the year in which you receive them.

FOUR TERMS TO REMEMBER

Dividends can make shareholders happy campers. But how and when they are received can be quite confusing. To clear the air, here are four terms investors of dividend-paying stocks must be familiar with:

- **Declaration date**   This is the day that the company's board of directors announces to the world that a) A corporate dividend is to be paid, b) How much the dividend will be, c) The payable date, and d) The record date.

- **Payable date**   This is the date that the company's dividends will be paid to all eligible shareholders.

- **Record date**   To be eligible to receive a company's dividend, shareholders must own the stock by this date. For example, if you bought shares of XYZ corporation on May 16, and the company is paying its dividend on May 31 to those with a record date of May 12, you must have purchased shares of that stock on or before May 12. Buying on May 16 means you missed the current dividend payout.

- **Ex-dividend date**   The ex-dividend date is the day on which the dividend is actually deducted from the price of the stock. Anyone buying stock on or after this date will not be eligible to receive a dividend payout from the company during this quarter. Ex-dividend dates aren't set by the company itself but by the National Association of Securities Dealers.

All Is Not Lost!   Buying shares of stock on its ex-dividend date doesn't mean you'll miss out receiving a dividend from that company forever; it just means you won't receive the one that's been declared for that quarter.

UTILITY STOCKS AS DIVIDEND PAYERS

One popular type of "widows and orphans" stock is *utility stocks*. Liked by investors because they provide a steady income stream, loved by brokers selling them because they can generally satisfy their clients' needs, utility stocks have often formed the foundation upon which many stock portfolios are built.

Today, however, utility stocks aren't all what they use to be. In the 1990s, a utility stock isn't necessarily just a plain-old gas, electric, or telephone company play. Often these companies are large conglomerates that own all sorts of other businesses, companies, or have a hand in the telecommunications industry. Consequently, assuming that all utility stocks are alike, or that the management of each is as dedicated to increasing dividends as many once were is no longer appropriate.

That's not to say these kinds of stocks aren't good investments. I'm merely pointing out that these companies—like others—need to be researched and, like the Oldsmobile, today's utility stocks aren't necessarily like the ones your father bought.

Calculating Dividend Yield   Figuring out a company's dividend yield is easy. All it takes is knowing the per share price you paid for the stock, how much in dollars and cents the dividend is, and the ability to divide.

For example, if Make Me Rich Corporation is selling for $50 a share, and the board of directors decides it's going to pay its common stock shareholders $2 a share in dividends, 2 divided by 50 equals .04. So, the stock is paying a dividend yield of 4 percent.

DIVIDEND REINVESTMENT PLANS

A *dividend reinvestment plan* allows participating shareholders to purchase more shares of the company's stock with the dividends they are paid. These plans are one of the niftiest ways to build a stock portfolio and not invest more money than you originally laid out for your initial shares of dividend-paying stocks. These plans are referred to as DRIPs or DRPs, and literally hundreds of companies offer them to their shareholders.

Depending on the company, or the way you decide to participate in a DRIP, it can take anywhere from the cost of one share of a company's stock to $10, $50, $100, or $1,000 to begin this investment plan.

As for the kind of money that can be made via DRIPs, according to *Standard & Poor's Directory of Dividend Reinvestment Plans,* if you had invested $1,000 in Coca-Cola in 1985 reinvesting the dividends from that stock all along the way, at the end of 1995 your investment would be worth $12,680. That's an average annual return of 29 percent over that 10-year period. On the other hand, a $1,000 investment into the footwear retailer Brown Group and reinvesting dividends all along, would only be worth $745 at year end 1995. That's an average annual rate of return of –3 percent. As those two examples show, there's risk in DRIP investing too.

Three easy ways to begin investing in a company's dividend reinvestment plan are:

1. Buy shares of a dividend-paying company offering a reinvestment plan as you would any other stock through your broker. Then, tell your broker you'd like to have that company's dividends reinvested, or paid to you in the form of additional shares of stock.

2. Join the National Association of Investors Corporation, (NAIC). Once all membership dues are paid, starting a DRIP program can begin with as little as one share of a company's stock. Their address is

NAIC
711 W. 13 Mile Rd.
Madison Heights, MI 48071
810-583-6242

3. Or, to research the DRIP arena on your own, look for the *Standard & Poor's Directory of Dividend Reinvestment Plans* in your library's reference section; ask your broker if his or her firm has a list showing the companies that offer dividend reinvestment plans; or contact the American Association of Individual Investors, AAII. This Chicago-based non-profit organization has plenty of information available on DRIPs.

In this lesson, you learned about dividend-paying stocks, utility stocks, and dividend reinvestment plans. In the next lesson, you will learn what to look for when buying shares of stock.

WHAT TO LOOK FOR WHEN BUYING STOCKS

In this lesson, you will learn how to evaluate a company before buying any of its shares of stock.

Now that you have learned about the stock markets and the various kinds of stock and their personalities, it's time to research individual companies to determine which stocks you'd like to invest in.

WHERE TO LOOK FOR STOCK IDEAS

There are plenty of places to get stock-investing ideas. Brokerage firms typically have lists of stocks that they have researched, recommend, and make available to prospective and existing clients. Newsletters are full of stock ideas, as are magazines, newspapers, online forums, the Internet, and books.

If none of those appeal to you, you really don't have to look any further than your own buying habits to come up with some dandy stock ideas. Instead of feeling stumped, or seeing the entire 9,000-plus universe of traded stocks as mind-boggling, remember that most of us have been consumers of products that we love and whose stocks have traded on the exchanges for years.

The Winn-Dixie grocery chain, for instance, has had a terrific long-term market history. It's even been paying dividends consistently since 1934. If you chew Doublemint gum, Wrigley's is another blue-chip company with a positive long-standing reputation. Shop at Target? That's owned by Dayton Hudson which trades on the NYSE. As you can see, investment opportunities exist nearly everywhere you look.

Stock Picks Made Easy If you're still stuck for which company to invest in, think about the bills you pay every month: at least one utility bill, a telephone bill, and a handful of store and bank credit cards.

Investing money where you already spend it is a good place to start: If you're hooked on a store, bank, or brand of shoes, thousands of others are probably purchasing those goods or using the same services. Why not investigate?

Understanding the Company and Its Products

After you hone in on some companies whose products you like, it's time to get practical and look at what makes a company tick. The most important thing any educated stock investor can do before buying a company's stock is to learn everything there is to know about that company. Some of the things you'll want to find out include

- All the company's products and services.

- Who its customers are, and who buys their products and services.

- Who or what is considered its competition.

- What kind of competitive edge the company has.

- What new products the company is working on.

- How much it spends on research and development each year.

- Whether the management has changed recently and why.

- How its stock has performed in the past.

- What their dividend paying policy is, and whether they have increased those dividends through the years.

- How much debt the company has.

- What its annual sales have been like in the past, what they are currently, and what the projected sales are for the future.

- Whether they are making a profit and if their future earnings potential is strong.

- Who is recommending the stock and why.

- Whether there are now, or have ever been, any serious legal problems facing the company.

- How *liquid* the company's stock is, or, how much of the stock trades daily.

Liquidity vs. Illiquidity   If you find what you consider to be a great stock that trades a small number of shares daily, better take a second look. Buying shares of an *illiquid* stock (one that doesn't trade much) means that filling your order could take days—not seconds as it does with stocks trading thousands of shares daily. Even worse, when it's time to sell shares of illiquid stock, depending on the timing and the number of shares you own, it could take days to sell the stock and you might not get the price you wanted.

TAKING A LOOK AT THE NUMBERS

If you're new to the world of stocks, picking a stock is one thing but looking at the company's balance sheet is quite another. For most, the sight of numbers and the sound of phrases like "price-earnings multiple" or "debt to equity ratio" is enough to make their eyes glaze over.

Fundamental Analysis vs. Technical Analysis
The difference between *fundamental stock analysis* and *technical analysis* is how you look at things. If you're interested in finding over- or undervalued stocks to invest in, you'll look at the fundamentals of a company, such as its earnings, sales, debt, income statements, and how their balance sheet reads.

Technical analysis is concerned with a company's stock price, the volume of shares that trade, and historical and market trends, too.

This section identifies a few of the most frequently quoted terms used in the fundamental and technical analysis of a stock.

Once you understand the meanings of each term, remember this: Beyond the definitions, there are no iron-clad rules or sure-fire formulas that guarantee that even the most positive fundamental or technical analysis of a company can provide you positive investment results.

Guaranteeing Results Through Stock Analysis   Don't count on a guaranteed return based on a company's fundamentals or its technical analysis. No matter how great a company's balance sheet, what its performance trends reveal, or how many shares are sold daily, you won't necessarily make money from that investment.

Timing, such as when you purchased a company's stock, when you sold it, and how the markets behaved during the interim, have just as much power in determining a stock's ability to make its investors money as its per-share price or balance sheet.

TERMS YOU NEED TO KNOW

Most of us don't have the interest, time, or education to do a truly thorough analysis of a company the way professional analysts and money managers do. But an understanding of the most important financial and balance-sheet terms can help you determine a company's basic well-being. Here are the most common:

- **Earnings Per Share, or EPS**   One of the most common ways to gain an understanding of a company's current and future growth is by looking at its EPS. The EPS is the portion of a company's net profit allocated to each share of stock. It's calculated by taking the amount of money a company earned in one year—after taxes and preferred shareholders and bondholders have been paid—and dividing that amount by the number of outstanding shares.

  If the MegaBucks Corporation has earnings of $5 million and 5 million shares outstanding, it would have an EPS of $1 per share (5÷5 = 1). An EPS that increases each year means that the company is growing. One that's steadily falling signals bad news and more research is necessary to find out why.

- **Dividend Yield**   The annualized percentage an investor earns from dividend payouts on their common and preferred stocks. It's figured by dividing the annual dividend per share by the current price of the stock. For instance, if My Lucky Day's stock is trading at $20 per share and the company is paying $1 per share per year in dividends, it would have a dividend yield of 5 percent ($1 divided by $20 = .05 or 5%).

- **Book Value**   A company's book value reflects—on a per-share basis—what a company's assets amount to after all intangibles have been deducted and all outstanding liabilities paid. Money pros compare a company's book value with its *market price* (what the shares of the company stock are currently selling for). Sometimes a company's market price is below its book value, which could mean that the company is trading for less than its net assets and therefore

might be a nice buy for value investors. Other times
the market price may be much higher than its book
value, which can often be the case with growth
stocks.

- **Price-Earnings Ratio, or P/E**   A company's P/E
  ratio represents the price of a stock divided by its
  earnings per share. In the case of My Lucky Day, if
  that stock is trading at $20 with earnings of $1 per
  share, 20 divided by 1 equals 20. So, its price earnings ratio would be 20.

Companies with high P/E multiples (today that's considered
over 20), are usually those of new, fast-growing companies.
Lower P/E ratio stocks are generally found in mature companies, and those that pay large dividends. One general investing
rule of thumb could then be, *The higher a company's P/E multiple, the riskier the investment.*

Incidentally, at the end of May 1996, the S & P 500 had a P/E
ratio of 19.8, according to the *Wall Street Journal.* In 1992, its
P/E ratio was 25.6.

- **Market Capitalization**   Market capitalization
  represents the dollar-value of a corporation's stock
  and is determined by multiplying the number of all
  the company's outstanding common shares of stock
  by the stock's current market price. So, if Big Money
  Corp. is trading for $50 a share, and has 100 million
  shares outstanding, it would have a market capitalization of $5 billion (100 million × $50).

  While there are no clear-cut industry definitions,
  some money pros consider a small-cap (small capitalization) stock to be one that has a market capitalization of under $500 million. Using the earlier
  example, Big Money Corp. would be a large-cap
  company.

- **Debt Ratio**   A company's debt ratio shows how much of a company's total capitalization is made up of long-term debt.

  To calculate it, take the total dollar amount of a company's outstanding bond debt and divide it by the company's total capitalization. So, if Big Money Corp. had $1 billion in bond debt and a bond value of $3 billion, it would have a debt to equity ratio of .33 or 33 percent (1÷3 = .33).

  Today, the average corporation has a debt ratio of about 33 percent.

- **Payout Ratio**   A payout ratio represents the percentage of net earnings a company uses to pay its dividend. Money pros say that a normal range for this ratio is between 25 and 50 percent of a company's net earnings. A higher ratio often signals that the company is struggling to meet its obligations, or it's a mature company with little growth opportunity.

- **Retained Earnings**   The net profit left after a company pays its dividends. It can also be called *undistributed profits* or *earned surplus*.

ANALYZING THE DATA

The financial information on a company will be most meaningful when you compare the data among like companies. This will put each stock in a better perspective and allow you to make a more informed decision about your investments.

One way to do that is to make a grid chart to have a visual example of how one company measures up against another.

Along the top line, make headings such as Price per Share, Dividend Dollar Amount, Dividend Yield, P/E Ratio, Number of Shares Outstanding, and so on—as much information as you want to compare. Then, list the companies you're interested in and fill in the chart. Hopefully, this will make it easier to find a company to put your money in. The worst thing that can happen is you'll learn a lot.

 Stay Focused   Before you make your first grid chart, make sure you are comparing apples with apples: growth companies with growth companies, and not a blue chip, dividend-paying company with a fast-growing high-tech company. Not comparing apples to apples means you'll draw inappropriate conclusions.

In this lesson, you learned about financial data and basic terminology that will help you evaluate a stock before you purchase it. In the next lesson, you will learn about other stock particulars not found in financial statements or balance sheets.

11

DON'T OVERLOOK THESE STOCK PARTICULARS

In this lesson, you will learn about stock particulars, including the effects of stock splits, and where you can look for statistical, informative and technical information about company stocks.

THE BUSINESS BEHIND STOCK OWNERSHIP

Once a stock is issued and is publicly traded, there are a few strategic business moves that a company can put into play that may or may not have a positive long-term effect on the per-share value of a stock but nonetheless are common business practice. Some of them include paying dividends in cash or stock, stock splits, stock repurchase programs, and rights offerings.

Here's what each means:

- **Dividends** As discussed in Lesson 9, dividends aren't guaranteed, are typically paid quarterly, and a company's board of directors decides what kind of dividend—cash or stock—is paid, along with when and how much.

If you're wondering how a dividend payment affects the per-share price of the company's stock, that depends—the value of the stock could increase, decrease, or not move at all.

For instance, if there is bad news surrounding a dividend payout, such as a company that always pays a dividend and decides not to, or reduces its dividend, that news will more than likely cause the per share price of the stock to fall. Then again, if a company decides to increase its dividend, the price of the stock could rise, thanks to the dividend boost.

Getting That Dividend   If you don't ever want to miss out on receiving a dividend, you first have to be a shareholder of record with that company.

That doesn't mean buying shares of company's stock on its ex-dividend date—that won't yield you the dividend. It means purchasing those stock shares at least five business days before the record date, if you'd like to receive it.

- **Stock splits**   There are two different kinds of stock splits a company may engage in: a regular *split* and a *reverse split*. One increases the number of shares you own. The other decreases it. A 2-for-1 regular stock split doubles the number of shares owned. For instance, if you owned 100 shares of Make Me Rich stock that trades for $50 a share, after the 2-for-1 stock split you'd hold 200 shares of the stock. Yippee!

But, just because the number of shares has increased doesn't mean the per share value of that stock—in dollars and cents—has increased. In the previous example, yes, you would have doubled the number of shares of the stock owned but the stock would be trading at half its value, or $25 a share instead of $50.

One reason companies declare stock splits is to keep their stock trading in a dollar range that investors find attractive—usually somewhere above $20 and under $100 per share.

Reverse stock splits are a strategy companies generally employ when the price of a stock is too low. Lower priced stocks, just like higher priced ones, don't have the curb appeal that those trading in the above $20 to under $100 range do. So, if you owned 500 shares of the Bold & Brassy Corp. and its stock was trading at $5 per share, if the company announced a 2-for-1 reverse split, you'd be the proud owner of 250 shares trading at $10 per share.

In both cases, a regular split or reverse split, the total dollar value of your investment doesn't change one iota: 100 shares times $50 per share equals $5,000 in market value. After the 2-for-1 split, 200 shares times $25 per share also equals a market value of $5,000.

When it comes to the reverse split the same is true: 500 shares of a $5 stock equals $2,500 in market value, as does 250 shares of a $10 stock.

Both types of splits then represent little more than bookkeeping entries. So, while the number of shares owned and the per-share price on those shares may change, investors aren't getting something for nothing when a split occurs.

As far as Wall Street is concerned, reverse splits are generally a bad deal, as the prices of the stocks experiencing a reverse split have historically had a tendency to decrease—not increase—in value.

* **Share repurchases**   A share repurchase happens
when a company decides to buy back shares of its
company stock. Two ways to do this are through a
formal tender offer, or to merely buy shares of the
stock in the open marketplace. The latter can happen
unnoticed by Wall Street if the amount of shares
purchased is small. Tender offers, however, are always noticed.

In a tender offer, the company is spending its own
money to buy back shares of its stock from its existing shareholders. To do so, the company must an-
nounce the offer, establish a tender price for the
stock, and put a time limit on the offer. To sweeten
the deal, the tender price is higher than the price the
stock is trading previous to the tender announcement; so shareholders wanting to sell shares of a
company's stock that has just announced a tender
offer would find that there's money to be made in
the short-term by liquidating their shares via a
company's tender offer. On the other hand, a tender
offer usually winds up bringing the per share price of
a stock up. So, deciding whether to take advantage of
this offer requires understanding...

All the ramifications of the offer.

The reasons why the company is buying back its
shares.

Your long-term investing plans regarding this
company.

Treasury Stock   Stock that a company buys back after it has already been issued is called *treasury stock*. Treasury stock doesn't have voting rights, doesn't receive dividends, and is not counted as outstanding stock when the company's earnings per share are figured.

- **Rights offerings**   Companies that want to issue new shares of their stock to existing shareholders may do so through a rights offering. It's a kind of "right-of-first-refusal" to buy that's offered shareholders—one that comes with price stipulations and a fixed date when the offer expires. And that's the good news. The bad news is, the market doesn't always care for rights offerings because the issuance of these new shares can dilute (water down) the number of shares owned. This in turn typically has a negative impact on the price per share because it increases the shareholder base and, if the company pays a dividend, means more shareholders to pay dividends to.

RELIABLE RESOURCES

You can find out about stock splits, repurchase programs, and all the other information discussed in this lesson through a variety of resources. First, as a shareholder in a company, any corporate news generally comes to you via the company through the mail, or it will come to you from your broker.

Both shareholders and non-shareholders alike will find the *Wall Street Journal, Investor's Business Daily,* and *Barron's* good places to start for finding up-to-date information about a stock. Plus, you will find periodic reports on dividends or earnings as they are released by the companies.

If you're computer-savvy, online services like America OnLine have all sorts of information about a company available to its subscribers. Brokers also have data about companies they can send to you.

The reference section of the library is another reliable source for stock data. Look for books like *Value Line Stock Reports* and the *Standard & Poor's Monthly Stock Guide*. Both supply plenty of individual stock information and will help in your research.

Writing or calling a company requesting their annual report and accompanying 10-K report makes good sense, too. Both contain detailed discussions that should give you a better understanding of the company's personality, and both pieces are free. You'll find a company's name, address, and phone number in the *Value Line Stock Reports*.

Annual Report and 10-Ks   The Securities and Exchange Commission requires all publicly traded companies to file and distribute an annual report and a 10-K report. The annual report, as its name suggests, comes out once a year and contains a report from the president, general business and performance data, financial statements and accompanying notes, and an auditor's report.

The 10-K discloses more detailed information about the company's business practices, sales agreements, the management's compensation, and the board of directors.

GOING ONLINE

If you don't have a home computer, your nearest library probably does, and using it is free. So, if you'd like to do some stock research on your own, the New Americas Information Group offers these tips on using your library's computers:

- Once you find your way to the Internet, type the name of the company you want to learn more about. Many companies have Web sites and from them you'll be able to glean lots of info, like company news and financial statements.

- The Securities and Exchange Commission (SEC) requires all public companies to file their financial documents electronically through a system named EDGAR. EDGAR's Web address is: **http://www.sec.gov/edgarhp.htm**.

- To check if a company is in bankruptcy, the Web address is: **http://bankrupt.com**.

- To get a quote on a company stock price, do this through PC Quote by entering: **http://www.pcquote.com**.

In this lesson, you learned about some of the particulars of stock investing along with some reliable resources to use when researching stocks on your own. In the next lesson, you'll learn about how to buy stocks.

12

HOW TO BUY STOCKS

In this lesson, you'll learn about buying stocks, paying commissions, investing on margin, and the different kinds of orders you may place when buying or selling stock.

Finding a company to invest in is only part of the investing story; other chapters begin when you try to decide how many shares of the stock to buy, when to buy them, when to sell them, how much commission you're willing to pay for your trades, and whether you'd like to work with a professional or be an independent investor making stock decisions based on your own research.

Throughout the following lessons, all of those issues will be addressed. But right now it's time to focus on the various amounts of stock you can purchase, and the kinds of orders for buying and selling stocks that you may place.

THE SIZE OF THE TRADE

Two common terms used in the brokerage business that relate to the size of a stock order that investors make are "round lot" and "odd lot." A *round lot* is equal to 100 shares of a stock, with one exception: 10 shares of a stock may be considered a round lot when the stock doesn't trade often. An odd lot is anything under 100 shares of stock, as in 1 to 99 shares.

One benefit of investing in round lots—excluding the one exception—is that commissions are generally cheaper on round lot trades than they are on odd lot trades. For instance, buying 100 shares of a stock at a brokerage firm might cost a commission of $50 for the trade. Buying 35 shares of the same stock from the same firm will—more often than not—cost the same $50. So, know in advance that you'll get more for your commission money when buying round rather than odd lots.

COMMISSIONS

Since we're on the subject, we should discuss *commissions*, as they play an integral part in your stock investing career. Commissions are part of the brokerage business and your investing life because the brokerage business is a sales-oriented one in which salespeople (brokers) earn income on a commission basis. Even if the word "commission" is not used and "fee-based" substituted for it, most brokers within the securities industry earn their income based on the commission generated by the volume and number of stock trades—or other security sales—they do. Or, they earn their money based upon the dollar amount of assets they control. The latter is referred to as "fee-based" and the more money a broker manages, the more money he or she can make.

Commissions are paid when you buy and sell stocks—with one exception: When purchasing an initial public offering of a stock, or IPO, there is no visible commission charged on that trade. The broker selling you that IPO, however, is not working for nothing. He or she is getting paid a fee for every share of the IPO sold. In reality then, the commission is built into the offering price of an IPO.

When it comes to commissions, it pays to shop around, because commission prices aren't fixed across the board as they were prior to 1974. Instead, there are securities firms that are called *full-service* firms and others referred to as *discount* firms. The difference between the two is commissions—at full-service brokerage houses the commissions are typically going to be higher than those at a discount brokerage house.

Another difference between discount and full-service firms is not the quality of service you'll receive, but rather, how much professional investing advice you'll get.

Most brokerage firms are staffed with well-educated, multi-licensed men and women selling securities. Therefore, the quality of the service between the discount and full-service brokerage firms, from a big picture point of view, is similar. One thing investors can expect from a full-service firm that they aren't likely to get as much of from a discount brokerage firm is investment advice, research data, and researched stock recommendations.

If you're wondering which is better, a full-service or discount brokerage firm, there is no one absolute answer to that question. Both have plusses and minuses. More on that subject in Lesson 13.

The Long and Short of It   Once you're a shareholder in a company, Wall Street lingo for owning a stock that you expect to increase in value over time is *long*. If you own 200 shares of Microsoft, for instance, you are long 200 shares of Microsoft.

On the other hand, you can be *short* a stock too. In this case you don't actually own the shares, you're engaging in an investment strategy in which you expect the price of a stock to fall. To take advantage of that hoped-for decrease, you sell a stock without actually owning it, but borrowing the shares from the broker. Then, when it's time to deliver the stock, you buy it back in the open-market at—hopefully—a lower price. If all goes as planned, you make money.

The Risks of Selling Short While the concept might sound simple enough, in reality, not too many wizards on Wall Street are masters of selling short. That's because it means you're betting the price of a stock will decline within a given period of time. And, while not all stocks always increase in value, the historic long-term trend on Wall Street has been an increase rather than a decrease in stock prices.

MARGIN

Margin is a way to invest with borrowed money, literally. It works like this: If you'd like to buy 300 shares of XYZ stock that sells for $30 per share, instead of having to pay the full tariff for that trade of $9,000, buying that stock *on margin* would mean only coming up with a fraction of the money and borrowing the rest from the brokerage firm you're doing business with. In today's markets, that would mean coming up with 50 percent of the market value, or $4,500.

Opening a margin account isn't for everyone. The rules governing these accounts are governed by the National Association of Securities Dealers (NASD), the New York Stock

Exchange, as well as the individual brokerage house you're doing business with. Plus, before you can open a margin account, you have to have at least $2,000 in cash or securities in your brokerage account.

Although margin accounts allow you to own more shares of stock for less money, stock certificates aren't sent to you but are kept in your account at the brokerage firm, and you may be called upon to add more money to your account should the value of the securities in it fall below margin requirements. This is called a *margin call*. So, the downside of margin accounts is that you may have to ante up more money, or sell shares of the stock you own, when money is needed to bring the value of their margin accounts up to the brokerage firm regulated amounts.

Margin Accounts and History   Before the stock market crash in 1929, people were able to buy shares with only 10 percent down, borrowing the other 90 percent on margin. Investors felt like royalty when prices were rising, but jumped out of windows when the market fell and they had to meet their margin call requirements.

WHAT KIND OF ORDER TO PLACE

Placing your first order to buy a stock can be a little intimidating. Once you open an account at a brokerage firm, giving your order to buy stock to the broker comes with questions, such as...

- The name of the stock you'd like to purchase.
- What class of stock you're interested in buying, such as the company's preferred or common shares.

- How many shares you'd like to buy.

- What price you are willing to pay for the shares.

The last question needs to be addressed, because there are a number of different ways to place a stock order, the two most common being a market order and a limit order.

A *market order* is the quickest and the most efficient way to place an order to buy—or sell—stock. Quite literally, market orders can be filled within seconds after received. And, when placing a market order, you know that your order will be executed at the lowest price available if you're buying shares of stock, or the highest bid price available if you are selling shares of stock.

Limit orders are those in which you have established a price at which your stock is to be traded. For instance, let's say you want to buy 300 shares of Florida Power and Light (FPL) stock, currently trading around $34 per share, and you aren't willing to pay more than $33 a share for it. To do so, you would place a limit order to buy 300 shares of FPL at $33 per share. If you were trying to sell 300 shares of FPL and wanted no less than say $35 per share for it, a limit order to sell 300 shares of FPL at $35 per share would be entered by the broker. In either case, the orders would not be filled unless the prices on each were met. Therefore, unlike a market order, there is no guarantee that a limit order will be filled because of the price restrictions set on them.

OTHER KINDS OF ORDERS

Two other kinds of orders are stop orders and stop-limit orders. Both are designed to protect, or lock in, prices on a stock. *Stop orders* turn into market orders once the stop price has been achieved. Here too, there is no guarantee that a stop order can or will be filled.

A *stop limit order* is a more explicit stop order. It adds another level of limits to the price at which a stock may be bought or sold.

For example, if you placed a stop limit order to buy FPL stock, it might read: Buy 300 FPL at 33 stop, limit 33 ¼. Translated, that means you are willing to buy 300 shares of FPL at $33 per share, then once the $33 per share is reached, if the order can't be fully executed, the maximum price you are willing to pay for their FPL shares is $33.25.

The difference between a stop order and a stop-limit order is that once the stop price is reached, a stop order ticket automatically becomes a market order. In the case of a stop-limit order, once the stop price is reached the order then becomes a limit order. Got that?

TIMING YOUR ORDERS

After you decide the kind of order you'd like to place and remember that the most efficiently executed ones are market orders, there are a number of timing procedures you can follow when placing your orders. Here are some of the most common ones:

- **Day order**   When you place a day order, your order is only good on the day you place it. If you enter an order to buy FPL on Monday, that order is only good for Monday. Period.

- **Good-till-canceled order or, GTC orders**
  Unlike day orders, GTC orders are good until the day they are canceled. Many brokerage firms automatically cancel GTC orders at the end of a month.

- **Fill-or-kill orders, or FOK orders**   Here the entire order must be filled immediately or the order gets canceled. So, if you hoped to buy 200 shares of Disney at $58 per share and Disney could not be bought at that price, the entire order would be canceled.

- **All-or-none orders, or AON orders**   Here too all of the order must be filled. If that can't be done, the order gets canceled. The difference between a FOK and an AON order is time. The FOK order has to be filled immediately. Specialists on the trading floors have more time to fill AON orders.

Keep It Simple   The best investing advice is to keep your investing strategies simple. If you've done your research, found a company you'd like to invest in, like the per share price range it's been trading at, place a market order for the stock.

Money pros advise new investors that it isn't always worth the hassle to try to save a 12 or 25 cents on 100 or 200 shares of a stock—especially if you plan on holding the stock for the long term.

TRANSLATING STOCK PRICES IN THE NEWSPAPER INTO REAL DOLLARS AND CENTS

FRACTIONS	DECIMAL EQUIVALENT	CENTS EQUIVALENT
1/16	.0625	6 cents
1/8	.1250	13 cents
3/16	.1875	19 cents

Fractions	Decimal Equivalent	Cents Equivalent
$\frac{1}{4}$	.2500	25 cents
$\frac{5}{16}$	.3125	31 cents
$\frac{3}{8}$	.3750	38 cents
$\frac{7}{16}$	.4375	44 cents
$\frac{1}{2}$	.5000	50 cents
$\frac{9}{16}$	.5625	56 cents
$\frac{5}{8}$	.6250	63 cents
$\frac{11}{16}$	.6875	69 cents
$\frac{3}{4}$	.7500	75 cents
$\frac{13}{16}$	.8125	81 cents
$\frac{7}{8}$	.8750	88 cents
$\frac{15}{16}$	.9375	94 cents

In this lesson, you learned about how to place orders and buy stocks. In the next lesson, you'll learn about where to buy stocks.

WHERE TO BUY STOCKS

In this lesson, you will learn about the different places stocks can be bought and sold.

Trading stocks has come a long way since the 18th and 19th centuries. Instead of buying and selling securities underneath a tree or on the curb of a street, today's investors can place their investment orders in one of two ways:

1. By going in-person to a brokerage house and conducting their investing business face-to-face.

2. Or, they can do their stock buying and selling over the telephone lines, either by placing phone calls to their brokerage firms or by using a modem to buy and sell stocks on their computers using the Internet.

Whatever avenue they choose, one of the first questions investors are faced with is understanding the differences between discount and full-service brokerage firms.

THE DIFFERENCE BETWEEN BROKERAGE FIRMS

As you learned in Lesson 12, there are two distinct types of brokerage firms: Full-service and discount brokers. The primary difference among them lies in their level of service. That is, the amount of investment advice you receive and the amount of money you pay for that advice.

At *full-service* brokerage firms, like Merrill Lynch or Smith Barney, expect to pay higher commissions for the securities transactions you conduct there. At discount brokerage firms, such as Jack White or Schwab, commissions won't be as high.

Before May 1, 1975, referred to in the brokerage world as May Day, there were no discount brokerage firms in the country. Instead, commissions were fixed and brokerage firms across the nation used the same rates. After May Day, firms were allowed to discount their commissions. That move created the split between discount and full-service firms.

WHAT IS A BROKER?

If you're wondering what a broker is, according to *The Wall Street Journal's Guide to Understanding Money and Investing*, originally a broker was "a wine seller who broached—broke open—wine casks. Today's broker has a less liquid but often heady job as a financial agent."

Cute definition—but no longer appropriate. Today, a stock broker is an individual who is licensed as a registered representative and thereby acts as an intermediary between a buyer and seller of securities. For their work, brokers are paid a commission.

FULL-SERVICE AND DISCOUNT BROKERS

Ideally, full-service brokers spend their time finding the right products for their clients, helping them create long-term investment goals, and giving financial and investment guidance and direction. Discount brokers aren't likely to be as investment goal-oriented as full-service brokers are, nor do their companies generally have the investment research that full-service firms do.

The line between the full and discount broker is narrowing, however. And in some cases, so is the spread between commissions charged.

If you are a relatively new or inexperienced investor, you may find the added services of a full-service brokerage firm beneficial. Your broker will have up-to-date research on individual companies that you may not have access to, and he or she can advise you as to which stocks are appropriate to meet your financial goals. Full-service brokers may also offer you other types of financial planning such as estate and tax information.

You can't always tell by the name whether a brokerage firm is a discount or full-service one. Nor is it wise to assume that just because a firm has a policy of charging full-service rates that it won't discount those commissions under certain conditions. Or, that all discount brokerage commissions are the same. There is plenty of competition among brokerage houses for your business. So, just like any other business in America, it pays to shop around for those looking for the lowest commission cost provider.

The following short list of brokerage firms will help familiarize you with some of the nation's best known firms and their commission fee status:

NAME OF BROKERAGE FIRM	COMMISSION STATUS
A.G. Edwards & Sons	Full-service
Charles Schwab & Co. Inc.	Discount
Dean Witter Reynolds	Full-service

NAME OF BROKERAGE FIRM	COMMISSION STATUS
Fidelity Investments	Discount
Gruntal & Co.	Full-service
Merrill Lynch	Full-service
Olde Discount Stockbrokers	Discount
Paine Webber	Full-service
Quick & Reilly	Discount
Smith Barney	Full-service

LOOKING FOR A DISCOUNT BROKER ONLINE?

If you're comfortable with computers and want to save some money when trading stocks, the Internet currently offers a number of discount brokerage firm choices.

The costs for setting up cyberspace accounts currently varies from $0 to around $50 depending upon the firm. The costs for stock transactions depends upon the brokerage firm selected, the amount of shares of stock purchased or sold and the price per share of the security. For instance, in early 1996, commissions on 100 shares of a $20 stock cost $55 at Charles Schwab and $19.95 at E*Trade Securities.

Along with a variety of fees, there can be costs for real-time and/or delayed time stock quotes, and limitations on the types of securities available at each firm and the types of buy/sell orders you'd like to place.

Looking for the latest list of online discount brokers? The Discount Brokerage Online Information Center, sponsored by the National Council of Individual Investors, has a Web site with the scoop. To access it, their address is: **http: //www.ncii.org/ncii.**

In the end, however, there seems to be a promising future for the stock transactions conducted in cyberspace. So, if you're hunting for online opportunities, here is a brief overview of some brokerage firms now doing business in the great beyond.

- **Charles Schwab**
  800-435-4000
  Product name: StreetSmart
  Systems supported: Windows, Mac
  Securities handled: stocks, bonds, load and no-load mutual funds, options, cash management account

- **E*Trade Securities**
  800-786-2575
  Product name: E*Trade Securities
  Systems supported: any PC
  Securities handled: stocks, bonds, load and no-load mutual funds, options

- **Fidelity Brokerage Services**
  800-544-8666
  Product name: Fidelity Online XPress
  Systems supported: DOS
  Securities handled: stocks, bonds, load and no-load mutual funds, options, cash management account, annuities, CDs

- **Jack White & Co.**
  800-233-3411
  Product name: Path Online
  Systems supported: any PC w/Internet
  Securities handled: stocks, options

- **Muriel Siebert**
  800-872-0711
  Product name: Siebert Online Services
  Systems supported: any PC
  Securities handled: stocks, bonds, load and
  no-load mutual funds, options, cash management
  account

- **Quick & Reilly**
  800-672-7220
  Product name: QuickWay
  Systems supported: any PC
  Securities handled: stocks, bonds, load and
  no-load mutual funds, options, cash management
  account, CDs

- **T. Rowe Price Discount**
  800-638-5660
  Product name: PC Access-BBS
  Systems supported: any PC
  Securities handled: stocks, no-load mutual funds,
  options

*(Source: American Association of Individual Investors (AAII), Comput-
erized Investing, January/February 1996, Volume XV, No. 1, pages
12-17.)*

In this lesson, you learned where to buy and sell stocks. In the
next lesson, you will learn how and when to sell stocks, and
the accompanying risks and rewards.

14

WHEN TO SELL STOCKS

In this lesson, you'll learn about the risks and rewards of selling the stocks that you own.

One of the toughest decisions many newcomers to stock investing face is when to sell! Part of the reason is that there's no shortage of people encouraging you to invest in stocks, but not when it comes to advice and direction for *selling* those stocks. In the end, most people face this decision either on their own or with less guidance and counsel than they might prefer. This is uncomfortable for some, because deciding which companies to invest in was such an ordeal that the thought of selling those securities brings shivers up their spines—and their stocks never get traded. For others, trading stocks day-in and day-out without investment advice from professionals is common practice.

INVESTOR PERSONALITIES

The type of investor personality you have can impact the timing of when you sell the securities you own. Below are three examples of different investor personalities, along with a brief description of each and how they handle selling their stocks:

- **The buy-'em-and-forget-'em-forever type**   These individuals marry their stocks. They purchase shares of a company thinking that they will own those stocks until death do them part, literally. When to sell their securities is never an issue: It's out of the question and unlikely to ever happen.

- **The can't-lose-a-penny type**   These folks invest in the stock market believing that the per share price of the stocks they purchase can never fall below the price they paid. These unrealistic investors don't want to believe that stock prices can both fall and climb, or that some investors have become richer thanks to their stock investments, and others have become poorer. Any time the can't-lose-a-penny folks find out that their stock has fallen in value, they often run to sell their stocks and then conclude that they aren't any good at investing and/or that the stock market is a rip-off. These folks sell when the prices on their stocks fall.

- **The target type**   These investors know all about goals and limits. They invest with purpose and see the stock market as a world that holds opportunity for those who know how to manage their financial affairs. The target-investor will sell when whatever goal the stock was purchased for is met, or when the per share price hits a certain level. For example, a target investor might buy 100 shares of This Is A Good One at $20 a share, and decide that when that stock's price moves 20 percent in either direction— up to $24 dollars per share or down to $16 dollars— that she will reevaluate why she purchased the stock and make another decision: She might set another target price for those securities, buy more shares, or sell all or a portion of the shares she owns.

The target investor doesn't marry a stock investment for life—although they may wind up owning the same security for most of their lives because they've reassessed its value again and again. Nor do they let their emotions rule their investing strategies. Instead, target investors look at Wall Street with a practical and calculating eye.

Bid, Ask, and Quote   If you call your broker and want to sell 100 shares of your Motorola stock, and it's 2 p.m. on September 9, 1996, your broker will tell you the *bid price* is 51½. Bid, then, is the price you would receive for your shares at that time if you decided to sell.

If you wanted to purchase shares of Motorola, you'd pay the *ask price*, which in this example at that time was 51⅝.

If you combine the bid and ask prices, you wind up with a *quote.* So, the next time you're shopping for prices, call your broker and ask for a quote on Motorola, and she'll give you both the bid and ask prices.

Joining Hands   Remember, when you invest in stocks, you're not in the stock-buying business, you're in the *money-making* business. Invest in companies you'd like to be in business with.

Reasons For Selling

Once you have an idea of the kind of investing personality you might have, there are a host of reasons to sell the stocks you own. Here are five of them:

1. **When you need the money.** Odds are you invested in the stock market to make money, and if you find yourself in a situation where you need cash, take advantage of your good fortune and sell some of your stocks.

2. **When a stock has been a dud, you have a better investment idea, or the reasons you bought the stock no longer hold water.** In an earlier lesson, I pointed out that educated investors make the best investors. Therefore, learning as much as possible about a company before you invest always makes sense. To that end, I suggested that you find out information such as what products the company makes; who its customers and competition are; what kind of competitive edge the company has and what new products or services it is developing; whether the management has changed recently and why or why not; how the stock has performed in the past; what their dividend paying policy is; how much debt the company has; what its annual sales have been in the past, are currently, and are projected to be in the future; whether they are making a profit and whether their future earnings potential is strong; if there are any legal problems facing them; and whether shares of the stock trade actively.

   If a stock hasn't performed to your expectations after a given period of time, go back and investigate

what's been happening. If you don't like the company any longer, or have a better investment idea,
sell the stock and go for your better idea.

3. **When your goals are met.** People invest for all
sorts of reasons. Some invest for long-term goals,
such as growing a nest egg for their retirement or
paying for their kids' college education. Others invest for shorter time frames with the same purpose—
to accumulate money to buy things or to invest in
other things. But, if you've invested with a specific
financial goal in mind and that goal's been met, why
not reward yourself by selling the stock and following through on that goal?

4. **When you can't sleep at night.** Not everyone
has the psyche to be a stock investor. The people for
whom the market bell does *not* toll are the savers—
the people who can't sleep knowing that the money
they've invested in stocks may be worth less tomor-
row than it was today. Savers don't want to put their
principal at risk. They prefer to have that principal
grow—even if it is only growing at passbook savings
rates—which today are about 2 percent a year.

5. **When the timing isn't right for you.** Once
you've done your homework and slept on the results,
let intuition be your guide. Many money managers
follow their intuitions regarding the buying and selling of securities and individuals with intuitive skills
are advised to do the same. Intuition is a gut feeling
that you probably can't quantify or qualify but is
nonetheless real. Using your intuition effectively
means trusting that feeling and knowing the difference between your intuitive feelings, your fears, and
your skepticism.

If none of those ideas appeal to you, go back and review the grid chart you made in Lesson 10. Compare the prices and analysis you collected on various companies then with how those stocks are performing today. The current figures could indicate whether it's time to sell one—or some—of your stocks.

INVESTING CLICHÉS

There are lots of clichés about when to buy and sell stocks. Some of them are...

- Buy on bad news and sell on good news.

- If the trend shows a stock price moving upward, why stop a moving train?

- Bears make money, bulls make money, but pigs don't.

- Trees don't grow to the sky.

Knowing which cliché will work for you depends upon your investment experience and your point of view. For instance, which cliché(s) do you think fit the following?:

- Intel Corp., the computer folks, (symbol INTC), has traded between $49^{13}/_{16}$ and $83^{3}/_{4}$ during the last 52-week period ending September 9, 1996. That's a 67 percent increase over one year. Looked at on a closer range, on May 23, 1996, INTC was selling for $70^{7}/_{8}$. On September 9, INTC it was trading at $81^{1}/_{4}$. That's up well over $10 per share, or an increase of almost 15 percent.

  If clichés were your guide regarding when to sell this stock, which one would you use—why stop a moving train, or, trees don't grow to the sky?

- ValueJet (symbol VJET) had its share of problems in 1996 due to the crash of one of its jets in May that year. For the 52-week period ending the first week of September 1996, that stock's price ranged from 4½ to 34¾. The day before the plane crash, VJET was trading around $13.69 per share. Over the next few months, the per share price fell into the $5 and $6 dollar range. And, by the second week in September it was selling for $12 per share. As an investor, would you follow the cliché and buy on bad news?

Even with the aid of clichés, there is no definitive answer regarding when to sell—or buy—your stocks.

 Where the Real Money Is It's not so much what you pay for a stock that counts; it's what you sell it for that really matters.

In this lesson you learned about selling stocks. In the next lesson you will learn about the tax consequences of selling securities.

-15-

TAX CONSEQUENCES

In this lesson, you will learn some of the tax consequences of selling your stocks.

Ben Franklin said it best in 1789 when he wrote, "In this world nothing is certain but death and taxes." And while none of us know our precise death dates, we all know that taxes are figured every year.

The issue of taxes is complicated because no two of us and our investment experiences are the same, nor do we all have the same income levels or tax write-off opportunities. That means the best tax advice for the stock newcomer is to consult your own tax advisor regarding how your stock trading will impact your year end tax picture.

To make sure you've got a working knowledge of some of the terms and topics you're likely to run across when discussing taxes with that professional, here are some terms you need to be acquainted with:

- **Taxable gain and/or loss**   Gains and losses both refer to the bottom line and answer the question of, has this investment made or lost you money.

  A *taxable gain* happens if the per share price of the stock you bought was higher when it was sold than when it was purchased. A *loss* reflects a stock that was sold at a lower per share price than it was bought at. In calculating either, don't forget your commission expenses.

Figuring a gain or loss takes simple subtraction skills. For instance, if you bought My Lucky Day stock for $35 a share and sold it for $63 dollars a share, you'd have a $28 per share gain on that stock. How long you owned the shares would determine the rate at which you would be taxed.

Long and Short-Term Gains   If you owned My Lucky Day stock for longer than one year, any gains made from its sale are considered long-term capital gains. Currently, they are taxed at a maximum rate of 28 percent.

But, if you owned that stock for less than one year and you sold it at a profit, that gain would be taxed at your regular income tax rate, which could be higher or lower than the long-term capital gains tax rate.

- **Writing off capital losses**   Just because your stock investment didn't make you any money doesn't mean it was a worthless investing experience. Each year you can deduct up to $3,000 of capital losses from your ordinary income. Plus, if your capital loss was more than that amount, you may carry forward the unused capital loss from one year to the next in $3,000 per year intervals. Or, you may use it against current and future short- or long-term gains.

So, let's say instead of My Lucky Day stock being a profitable investment, it turned out to be a dog, and this stock you purchased for $35 a share, you sold at $5 a share. All would not be lost—you'd still have $3,000 in capital losses to use.

Keeping Records   It's not uncommon to buy more of a stock you like. When you do, remember that every time you acquire more shares the cost basis for it may change. A *cost basis* is the price you pay per share plus any commission costs. And, the length of time you hold those shares will be different from the original batch. Both of these facts mean keeping records is very important.

To maximize the benefits of stock investing—which includes selling shares of stocks when they provide the biggest tax advantage—set up a filing system for each stock you own. Label each folder by stock name and symbol, and keep all statements and confirmations showing when, where, and how much stock you purchased. Segregating your stock investments will be a snap and finding out a stock's cost basis all the easier.

- **Wash sale**   A wash sale is buying and selling the same stock simultaneously or within 30 days. If doing so results in a loss because of IRS rules, you can't use that loss on your taxes. So, a wash sale has no tax-advantages.

- **Tax-deferred accounts**   Stocks held and traded in tax-deferred accounts such as an IRA or 401(k) enjoy the luxury of delaying the payment of taxes due until a later date. Remember, tax-deferred is not

the same as *tax-free*. In tax-deferred accounts, taxes
are merely postponed, not eliminated.

PAYING TAXES

No one loves paying taxes. It's interesting how often investors
complain to their stock brokers about the amount of money
their investments made and the taxes they have to pay as a
result of their good fortune. For the record, making money is
the reason most people are drawn into the stock market, and
taxing the money we make has been part of our government's
system for decades.

For all who have made money from their stocks and want to
minimize their tax bite, consider these strategies:

1. If you've got a capital gain in a stock that you sold,
   look for some stocks that could be sold for a loss in
   your portfolio, sell them, and use those losses to offset the capital gains.

2. If you sold your stocks at a loss and don't have any
   gains to use those losses against, you can write off up
   to $3,000 in losses each year. Losses over that
   amount can be carried forward and used in the next
   year.

In this lesson, you learned about taxes and that the best tax
advice anyone can give you is to see your personal tax advisor
or consultant. In the next lesson, you will learn about various
investment strategies.

16

INVESTMENT STRATEGIES

In this lesson, you will learn 10 investment strategies that could enhance the value of your stock portfolio.

Once you become familiar with the ins and outs of stock investing, the next step for those who want to become more savvy investors is to strategize—employ some investment techniques that allow you to dance a little with the investments you made and hopefully increase your returns from them.

Investment strategies are not a part of the average investor's life. Most investors, especially those new to the market, are satisfied first learning how to invest and then building a portfolio of stocks. A minority actually moves on to use investment strategies such as market timing, option writing, selling short, or hedging their investments.

Here's a look at how missing some of the best days in the market, as represented by the S & P 500, has affected investment returns in the past. The chart reflects a 5-year time span ending December 31, 1995.

INVESTMENT PERIOD STATUS	AVERAGE ANNUAL PERCENT RETURN
fully invested	16.5%
missed 10 best days	11.1%
missed 20 best days	7.3%
missed 30 best days	4.2%
missed 40 best days	1.4%
missed 60 best days	–3.4%

 Market Timing   Getting out of the market when it's high and back in again when it's low is an investment strategy few master. And not only have few mastered it, but being out of the market and missing market highs often translates to missing money-making opportunities. So, as investment strategies go, staying fully invested for long periods of time can pay off more than hopping in and out of the market.

The rest of this lesson will address 10 common investment strategies used today. They are listed in numerical order with the lower numbers representing the simpler investment strategies and the highest numbers the more complex.

10 POPULAR INVESTMENT STRATEGIES

1. **DRIPs**   In Lesson 9 you learned about dividend reinvestment plans, or DRIPs as they are commonly called. For the new investor, who doesn't have a lot of money to invest and wants to create a diversified

portfolio and see the number of shares they own in a company grow almost magically, DRIPs can be a strategy worth pursuing.

Once you purchase shares of a company that offers shareholders the opportunity to use their dividend to purchase full and fractional shares of its stock, and enroll in that company's dividend reinvestment plan, each time the company pays a dividend, instead of receiving a cash dividend you'll be buying more shares of stock.

More than 900 companies now offer dividend reinvestment plans, most of which are large cap, blue chip firms.

Downsides to this investment strategy include taxes (DRIPs are taxed as dividends even though you're buying more shares of stock); selling your stocks is often time consuming because most investors don't take physical possession of their DRIP stock certificates, so selling these stocks isn't as easy as picking up the telephone and instructing your broker to do so because there is paperwork involved; and there's no investment advice for DRIP investors—you pick and choose the companies you'd like to invest in without the aid of a broker or financial planner's advice.

2. **Selecting small cap companies vs. larger cap ones** While the more conservative investment strategy is centered around blue chip companies— those firms that are well-established and often dividend paying ones that have been around so long almost everyone knows their names—the smaller cap companies return the highest rewards over the long-haul.

According to Ibbotson, a Chicago-based securities research firm, if you had invested $1,000 in large cap stocks in 1925, reinvesting all dividends and excluding taxes, by year-end 1995 you'd have $1,113,920. But, if you'd invested the same $1,000 in smaller companies, you'd have over $3.8 million.

Small cap companies, while riskier and typically not dividend paying, can offer more bang for the buck to investors who are willing to take on more risk.

3. **Dow dividend investing**   Here's a simple little strategy that has paid off royally over the years. In its original form it works like this: Look at all 30 of the stocks that make up the Dow Jones Industrial Average (Lesson 20 has a complete list of these companies); find the 10 companies paying the highest dividend yields; buy equal amounts of these 10 highest-yielding stocks—affectionately referred to as the "Dogs of the Dow"; hold them for one year; sell them; then recalculate and invest again.

From that investing strategy have come two others. One is, once you cull the 10 highest-yielding stocks in the Dow, glean the five with the lowest per share price; eliminate the lowest price stock from that group; then buy equal amounts of the four remaining stocks. Hold those stocks for one year, sell them, and begin the strategy all over again.

According to *Smart Money* magazine, this strategy has doubled the market returns annually over the past 25 years.

Another variation of the Dow dividend investing strategy is to buy the 10 lowest-yielding Dow stocks in equal amounts. Hold them for one year, sell, then recalculate and invest again.

If you can't afford to invest in all of the Dow stocks, there are unit investment trusts (UIT) that allow investors to invest in Dow dividend investment strategy programs with as little as $100 to $1,000. For more information about UITs, contact your broker or financial planner.

4. **Dividend paying stocks for income**   According to *Retire with Money*, a newsletter from the editors of *Money* magazine, of the 9,100 stocks traded on the exchanges only 21 have raised their dividends each year for 40 years or more. Investing in companies with a long-term history of not only paying dividends but increasing them is a strategy that may appeal to the fixed-income investor.

   What's attractive about this strategy is the historic dividend income these well-known blue chip companies have provided their shareholders. What's risky is that there is no guarantee that the dividends will continue—or continue to increase—in the future. Nor is there a guarantee as to how the company's stock price will perform.

 Not Piggly-Wiggly   Looking for the company with the best long-term record of increasing its dividends? The answer is: Winn-Dixie.

5. **Adding international stocks to a portfolio**
   Statistics show that over the long run, a portfolio made up of both international and U.S. stocks can beat the performance of a stock portfolio of only U.S. equities, and can even minimize volatility. The reason is that not all markets around the world perform

in sync—if stocks in the U.S. markets are having a rough year, those in the European or Far East markets might not be.

Some money pros recommend a blend of 30 percent international and 70 percent U.S. equities. If that 30/70 split is too much for you to swallow, there's no law against starting off small, perhaps allocating 5 to 10 percent of your assets to international stocks. The trick here, as in all market situations, is to pick the right stocks, at the right time, in the right markets.

6. **Options: Covered Call Writing**   Here's a relatively conservative investment strategy with probably one of the worst reputations around. This investment strategy requires that you own round lots of a stock, (a round lot is 100 shares), and asks that you not be emotionally married to your stocks. If you can agree to those terms, writing covered calls on the stocks you already own can provide you with added income from your investments.

To understand how this strategy works, you must understand what options are, how they work, and of what benefit they might be to you. One of the best sources for learning about options is the Options Industry Council. This organization has educational material that is easy to read and understand. You can contact them at:

**The Options Industry Council
440 South LaSalle St., Suite 2400
Chicago, IL 60605**

Ask specifically for their video entitled, "How to Optimize Your Stock Portfolio with Options," the brochures entitled "Understanding Stock Options" and "Characteristics and Risks of Standardized Options," and copies of their newsletter, *The Blueprint.*

Keep in mind, before any investor can participate in the options markets, they must first sign a paper stating that they have read the brochure entitled, "Characteristics and Risks of Standardized Options."

This brochure can be obtained through your broker or from The Options Industry Council.

OPTION Q & A

Let's take a breather for a moment to learn some of the basics of the world of options.

Q: What are options?

A: Options, as the name clearly implies, are investment strategies that give investors choices, affording them the opportunity to do more with the stocks they own than merely hold them. Technically, an option is a contract that gives its holder the right—but not obligation—to buy or sell shares of a stock at a specific price on or before a specific date.

Q: How many different kinds of stock options are there?

A: Two: calls and puts. A *call option* gives its holder the right to buy a stock at a specific price on or before a specific time. A *put option* gives its holder the right to sell a stock at a specific price or before a specific time.

Q: Why do people like options?

A: Because they provide opportunities. For investors who own stocks, writing covered call options, for instance, provides them with additional income from the stocks they own. In a down market, employing that strategy can mean making money when even when the stock price may not be moving upward. Buying puts, on the other hand, allows investors to do things such as protect the profits they have in the stocks they own.

Q: What's the toughest part of understanding options?

A: Keeping the jargon clear in your mind. The vocabulary of the options world is wild and wacky. You now know what puts and calls are, but there at least a dozen other terms you need to know if you are going to play the options game successfully. Three of the most common are:

> **strike price**   This is the stated price per share that a stock may be purchased for in the case of a call, or sold at, in the case of a put.

> **premium**   The premium is the price of an options contract that the buyer of the option pays to the options writer.

> **expiration date**   This is the last date that an options contract can be exercised. For stocks, the expiration date is the Saturday following the third Friday of the month that the option expires in. The longest length of time for standard options contract is three months.

Q: What are LEAPS?

A: LEAPS is an acronym for Long-term Equity AnticiPation Securities. The latest in options products, LEAPS contracts have expiration dates extending out three years.

7. **Buying uncovered calls**   If you think a company's stock is going to increase in value within the next few weeks or months and you don't want to ante up the full cost of 100 shares but do want to be a part of the stock's upward price movement, one

way to accomplish that is to buy *uncovered call contracts* on that stock. One options contract is equal to 100 shares of stock, and sells for a fraction of the cost of 100 shares of the stock. The cost for each contract is called *premium.*

The worst thing that could happen is that the stock does not move up in price as you hoped, your option expires, and you lose the premium—the amount of money it cost to purchase the contract(s)— plus, the cost of your brokerage commission fees.

On the upside, the stock could move up in price and, time permitting, so could the value of your call option. If that's the case, you could a) Sell your contract(s) before the option expires and pocket the profit, or b) If you'd like to own the stock and its per share price is higher than its strike price—this is called "being in the money"—you could exercise the option and buy the stock at its specified *strike* price— the stated price the stock can be purchased for. Depending on the contracts and commissions costs, you could wind up buying the stock for fewer dollars per share than what it's currently trading at in the market.

8. **Hedging** This investment strategy is used to offset the risk of losing money on your stocks in a declining market. One way to protect against falling prices on stock you own is to buy a put option. They work like this: Let's say you own 100 shares of XYZ corporation, which is currently $50 a share, and you're afraid the market is going to dive. To keep from losing money in that stock, you would buy one put option at a strike price of $50, and pay a premium for it.

That put option gives you the right to sell that stock at $50 per share over the next few months. Should that stock fall to say $45 per share during the life of the option, you could exercise your option and sell your 100 shares for $50 each. The cost of this hedging strategy is two-fold; first, there is the cost of the premium, and second, because you exercised your option, you no longer own the stock.

The hedgers in the world are primarily made up of the big institutional market players, like mutual fund portfolio managers and pension fund managers. Not many individual investors are hedgers.

9. **Selling short**   Another investment strategy employed by relatively few individual investors but numerous institutional investors is *selling short*. "Short" means you don't own the stock. "Long" means you do. So, if you own 100 shares of The Grass Is Green stock, a Wall Street way of referring to that stock position would be to say that you are "long 100 Grass Is Green".

If you're selling stock short, you aren't actually placing an order with your broker to buy stocks, you're placing an order with them to borrow stock. So, let's pretend that you know that the Grass Is Green Corp. is having some big problems and you anticipate that their stock, which is now selling for $65 a share, is going to fall.

To make money from the expected hardships at Grass Is Green, you would place an order to *sell short* 100 shares of it from your broker, pay the commission on the trade, then wait for that stock to drop in price. Assuming your information was accurate, and

the Grass Is Green goes from $65 a share down to
$30, you would place an order with your broker to
cover your short position which means that you
actually would buy the stock and give it to the brokerage firm that lent the stock to you.

In this case, you'd make $35 per share, less commis-
sions, from this strategy. The downside, however, is
if the stock does not fall but stays the same or rises.
In the latter two instances, you still have to cover
your short position and return the stock—which
could, depending upon the upward price movement—be very costly.

The *Wall Street Journal* keeps tabs on the amount of
short selling activity in a section of the paper called
"Short Interest Highlights." That's one place to find
out what other investors are thinking about the
market's direction and their expectations of down-
ward price movements on various stocks.

10. **Arbitrage**   Arbitrage is the simultaneous buying
    and selling of the same security in different markets.
    The profits made from this strategy come as a result
    of the price disparities between markets.

    An arbitrageur then, needs to have many eyes, be
    quick to move, and have the keen ability to coordi-
    nate the buying and selling of the same security in
    many markets simultaneously. You'll find arbitrag-
    eurs trading in currencies and commodities more
    often than in individual stocks.

In this lesson, you learned about some investment strategies.
In the next lesson, you will learn all about asset allocation.

17

MUTUAL FUNDS

In this lesson, you will learn what mutual funds are, why millions of people invest in them, what types of stock funds are available, and how to track funds.

In the late 1960s it was hard to give shares of mutual funds away. Yes, funds were around—mutual funds have been for sale in the United States since the mid 1920s—they just weren't very popular with the investing public. Today, all of that has dramatically changed. There are now easily twice the number of mutual funds in the marketplace than number of stocks listed on the New York Stock Exchange. In other words, mutual funds have been discovered, and one in three U.S. households owns shares in them.

WHAT IS A MUTUAL FUND?

Take a few dozen securities, such as stocks or bonds, package them in a single product that has an investment goal and allows people like you and me to purchase or redeem shares of them on any business day, and you've got a mutual fund.

Mutual funds are investment companies, and investment companies are mutual funds. According to the Investment Company Institute (ICI), the trade association for the mutual fund industry, a mutual fund is a company that makes investments on behalf of people or institutions who all share the same financial goal. The fund pools the money they receive from investors of the fund, then professional money managers use that pool to buy a variety of stocks, bonds, or money market instruments that they think will meet the investment objectives of the investment company or mutual fund, and of those who have invested in it.

WHAT DO FUNDS OFFER?

Mutual funds offer investors a variety of features, including

- An opportunity to invest into a diversified portfolio of securities.

- An investment in which the initial cost can range anywhere from under $100 to a few thousand dollars.

- The opportunity to invest in a product that is professionally managed.

- The opportunity to invest in literally dozens of different fund types—from growth to aggressive growth funds, bond funds, and money market mutual funds.

- The opportunity to invest in a liquid security.

On top of those features, some funds have made their shareholders plenty of money over the years. For example, the average annual return for a general U.S. stock fund over the past five years (from September 19, 1991 to September 19, 1996) has been 14.05 percent, according to Lipper Analytical Services, Inc. Over the last 10 years, U.S. stock funds had an average annual return of nearly 13 percent—12.96 percent, to be exact. So, while stock funds on average were returning double-digit returns to their shareholders, bank savings accounts were returning around 2 and 3 percent a year.

The top three performing funds among all the various types of stock funds over the past 5- and 10-years have been, according to Lipper:

FUND NAME	FIVE YEAR (9/91 TO 9/95)	FUND CATEGORY
Fidelity Select	34.61%	Science & Technology Electronics
Fidelity Select Home	32.43%	Financial Services Finance
PBHG Growth Fund	31.44%	Capital Appreciation
	TEN YEAR (9/86 TO 9/96)	FUND CATEGORY
20th Century GifTrust	23.51%	Small Company Growth
PBHG Growth Fund	23.09%	Capital Appreciation
Seligman Communications & Information	22.40%	Science & Technology

What You See   Don't expect the mutual fund performance results you see published in newspaper or magazine ads to be the exact returns you'll get from your fund picks. Performance results are yesterday's news. They are in the past. History. Kaput.

The kind of investment returns you'll get from your fund investment begin racking up the day you first invest your money and end the day you sell your fund shares.

FUND TYPES

There are zillions of investment choices to make when it comes to mutual funds. One reason there are so many choices is that the universe of funds is a huge one: At year-end 1995, Lipper Analytical Services reported that there were over 8,504 different open-end funds to pick from.

Another reason for the large number of funds is the investing public likes mutual funds and have made them popular products. And the third reason for so many funds in the marketplace is competition.

 Open-End and Closed-End Mutual Funds   An *open-end fund* is the type of mutual fund investors are most familiar with. Open-end means the shares are issued on demand. That means, unlike common stocks, in which a specific number of shares are issued, open-end funds issue shares as needed. They redeem those shares upon request also. So, if you want to buy 1,000 shares of Ain't She Sweet Aggressive Growth fund, no matter how many other shares have been issued, you can invest and become a shareholder—no ifs, ands, or buts.

But, if Ain't She Sweet was a common stock and not a mutual fund, for you to buy shares would mean someone else has to sell their shares.

Closed-end funds, however, are similar to common stocks. Only a specific number of shares are issued, and like common stocks, closed-end funds trade on major stock exchanges—like the New York Stock Exchange.

The Differences Among Funds

One thing that distinguishes one fund from another is its *investment objective*—the reason the fund was created. It also provides the basis for how money placed into that fund is invested. A fund with an investment objective of growth, for example, invests its money in growth stocks. A fund with an investment of income might invest its assets in fixed-income products such as corporate bonds, CDs, or preferred stocks.

The ICI identifies 21 different categories of funds based upon the fund's investment objective. They include: aggressive growth, growth, growth & income, precious metals, international, global equity, income-equity, flexible portfolio, balanced, income-mixed, income-bond, U.S. government income, Ginnie Mae, global bond, corporate bond, high-yield bond, national municipal long-term bond, state municipal long-term bond, tax-exempt money market national, tax-exempt money market state, and taxable money market funds.

While funds are typically classified by investment objective, some companies, firms, and publications that provide mutual fund data and performance results disagree on how they classify fund types. So, because there are no carved-in-granite fund classifications within the $3 trillion plus mutual fund industry, potential fund investors need to do their homework and read a fund's prospectus to find out why, where, and how the fund plans on investing their money. And then, make sure they select a fund they believe in and whose investment objective they agree with.

 Fund Family   When you hear names like Fidelity, INVESCO, AIM, Pioneer, or T.Rowe Price, you're hearing family names, sort of like the last names we all have.

But, when you hear the name Magellan, or Constellation, or Washington Mutual, you are hearing the names of individual funds.

So, if you think of a mutual fund family's name as you would a person's last name, and the name of a specific fund as you would someone's first name it will be easy for you to see that—like each of us—a mutual fund is a unique entity that stands on its own but also belongs to a family.

WHERE TO GO FOR FUND RESEARCH

The three most popular mutual fund research firms are Lipper Analytical Services, Morningstar, and Value Line. Each of these companies provides data about funds, but not all in the same fashion.

Lipper, for example, is best known for the performance rankings of funds—you'll see Lipper's fund performance numbers quoted in newspapers such as *The Wall Street Journal*. Morningstar, on the other hand, gives each fund a star rating. Morningstar caught the attention of the investing public with its easy-to-read one-page reports, which in turn have helped to make that company popular in providing user-friendly fund research. Value Line, provides a similar easy-to-read one-page mutual fund report for investors.

You will find one, if not all of these resources, along with other fund research from companies like Standard & Poor's and CDA/Wiesenberger, in the reference section of your library.

Keep in mind that even among the most respected fund-research companies, the fund you're doing research on may not be classified under the same heading in each publication.

Net Asset Value (NAV) and Offering Price A mutual fund's *net asset value* (NAV) represents the per-share market value of the fund's total assets, minus its liabilities, and divided by the total number of outstanding shares in the fund.

NAVs are figured daily, and as a result can change daily depending upon how the value of the securities in the fund's portfolio change, how the number of shareholders in the fund change, or because of a little bit of both.

When looking up fund data in a newspaper, you'll see "Offering Price" and "NAV." A fund's *offering price* represents the NAV plus the maximum sales charge the fund can charge

The next time you read the mutual fund pages, notice that no-load funds have no offering price—they carry no sales charges. Only load funds do.

 Finding Fund Data Investors can't always count on the classification of mutual funds to be the same when they are looking for fund data in newspapers, magazines, or even from firms dedicated to providing fund info. To overcome these discrepancies, make sure you:

- Know the exact and full name of the mutual fund(s) you invested in.

- Search for your fund data by name first and investment object second.

- Read the fund's prospectus thoroughly to find out the fund's investing particulars.

LOADS AND NO-LOAD FUNDS

A *load* refers to the sales charge that some mutual funds have. A sales charge is akin to a commission; it represents where and how the person selling you a fund gets paid for their efforts. *No-load* mutual funds have no sales charges.

It would be nice if discussing the sales charge on mutual funds was simple—but it isn't. There are differences in the amount of sales charges load funds charge, and also in the purity of fees that no-load funds charge.

In an effort to simplify the sales charge issues, different classes of stock have been issued for mutual funds—each representing various kinds of ways to pay a company's sales charges. Here's a look at the three most common classes of fund stock:

CLASS OF SHARES	SALES CHARGE	HOW IT WORKS
Class A shares	front-end load	a one-time fee paid before the actual fund investment has been first made
Class B shares	back-end load often called CDSL (contingent deferred salesload)	all money gets invested right away and the sales charges are taken out when selling shares; charge could disappear if you own shares long enough
Class C shares	no front-or back-end fees but an ongoing annual fee called a 12b-1 charge that ranges between 1–2% annually and has a lifetime cap of 8%.	no moneys taken out for sales charges

> **!** **Nobody works for nothing** There are no free lunches in the world of mutual funds—even when investing in no-load funds. One fee all fund investors pay every year—no matter what class of fund shares they own, type of no-load fund they've invested in, or 12b-1 fees they're exposed to—is the fund's *annual expense fees*. This fee is presented as a percent, expressed as a ratio, and calculated based on the fund's net assets. A typical expense ratio ranges from 0.75% to around 2% per year. Funds with annual expense ratios higher than 2% are considered expensive. The average expense ration is about 1.5 percent.
>
> Look for a fund's annual expense ratios and annual fees on page 3 of its prospectus.

BUILDING A MUTUAL FUND PORTFOLIO

Building a mutual fund portfolio is a lot like building a stock portfolio—each begins by knowing yourself, your risk tolerance, your reasons for investing, and how long you intend to stay invested.

So, while there are no pat formulas for creating a mutual fund portfolio, depending on your age and stage in life, pros suggest fund portfolios that contain a blend of money market funds, stock, and bond funds. The guidelines suggested are basically the same ones you use when you create a diversified investment portfolio; you decide the asset allocation in each based on your needs.

Also, to make things easier for their investors, fund families have created *asset allocation funds*. These funds can also be called *lifestyle* or *life-stage funds*, and will change their portfolio compositions depending upon changes in market conditions.

To help understand the variable risks among stock mutual funds, here's a glance at a few fund types and a broad generalization of the level of risk associated with each:

TYPE OF STOCK FUND	LEVEL OF RISK
Money market mutual funds	Least risky
Blue chip stock funds	Low risk
Small cap stock funds	Higher risk
Specialty fund or single country funds	Highest risk

Starting Out   One way to get your feet wet in the mutual fund arena is to begin your fund investments with a money market mutual fund. When you're comfortable with that investment, you might want to move on to an index fund.

An index fund is designed to perform as the index it follows does. So, since few stock funds historically outperform the S & P 500 index, investing in a fund that tracks that index could make good sense. Don't think, however, that index funds won't be volatile. The gains and losses on indexes move up and down a lot over time—and your fund will too.

TRACKING YOUR FUND

The best way to pick a winning fund and get rid of a losing one is to look at how the fund performs in relationship to its peers and the index of stocks that the fund has the most of in its portfolio.

To do that, you have to know a couple of things. The first is what your fund invests in, which you'll find out by reading the fund's prospectus and its annual report. Then, once you know the kind of securities the fund buys, you'll be able to find an index of similar stocks and look at the performance of other like funds.

For instance, a stock fund made up of blue-chip stocks might use both the DJIA and the S & P 500 as benchmark comparisons. Whereas one that invests in emerging company and/or small-cap stocks would look at NASDAQ when comparing returns. Lesson 20 is all about the various indexes.

Lipper Analytical Services is the only tracking company that has created a number of indexes, each made to follow a specific type of fund. You'll find the Lipper Indexes in *The Wall Street Journal* and *Baron's*.

In this lesson, you learned about mutual funds. In the next lesson, you will learn about getting financial advice.

18

INDEXES THAT TRACK STOCKS AND MUTUAL FUNDS

In this lesson, you will learn about the various stock market indexes and averages, and how to use the information to track your investments.

WHAT IS AN INDEX OR AVERAGE?

When you own stocks or mutual funds, the best way to find out how your investments are performing is to compare their performances with that of various indexes. Depending on the kind of securities you own and for proper comparisons, you will want to select the appropriate index or average so that you will be comparing apples to apples and not apples to oranges.

 Average and Index While there are some technical differences between an "average" and an "index," most people consider them one and the same. However, an *average* is an arithmetic mean that represents selected securities and is used to show how the overall market is performing. The most familiar stock market average is the Dow Jones Industrial Average.

continues

continues

An *index* is an average that reflects changes in something with an already established value.

Investors today use both as benchmarks when they try to see how their investments measure up against the broader indexes and/or averages.

HOW CAN THE AVERAGES HELP ME?

Indexes and averages are important tools for comparison because they:

- **Are easily found.** Most local newspapers and financial publications, such as the *Wall Street Journal*, show how the markets have performed daily using indexes like the Dow Jones Industrial Average or NASDAQ.

- **Show historical trends.** Along with the index, trend graphs are often made to show the direction of the index or average over a specific time period.

- **Provide a way for you to evaluate the performance of your own portfolio.** If the Dow Jones Industrial Average (DJIA) is up 20 percent for the year and you own a blue-chip stock that's up 35 percent, using the average to compare results makes it easy to see that your investment is performing better than the weighted average of the 30 blue-chip companies that make up the DJIA.

HOW DO I KNOW WHICH INDEX TO USE?

There are dozens of different indexes and averages around. The trick is finding the ones made up of the kinds of stocks you're investing in. For example, if you're a small cap stock investor, using the DJIA to get an idea of how your company is performing in relationship to other small cap stocks wouldn't make any sense. That's because the DJIA is made up of large blue-chip companies. A better choice would be the NASDAQ Small Cap Issues or the Russell 2000 Small Stock Index.

To help you understand the different indexes and averages, here are descriptions of some of the most widely used stock market averages and indexes:

- **Dow Jones Industrial Average (DJIA)** The Dow is the most common stock market indicator and is comprised of 30 major U.S. industrial companies. This is the average most frequently quoted at the end of each business day and represents the so-called "blue-chip" stocks.

THE DOW 30

AT&T	Du Pont
Allied Signal	Eastman Kodak
Alcoa	Exxon
American Express	General Electric
Bethlehem Steel	General Motors
Boeing	Goodyear
Caterpillar	IBM
Chevron	International Paper
Coca-Cola	McDonald's
Disney	Merck

Minnesota Mining	Texaco
J.P. Morgan	Union Carbide
Philip Morris	United Technologies
Procter & Gamble	Westinghouse
Sears Roebuck	Woolworth

Source: Barron's, *August 19, 1996*

- **Dow Jones Transportation Average** This average tracks 20 stocks in the transportation industry, including airlines, railroads and trucking companies.

- **Dow Jones Utility Average** This average follows 15 gas, electric, and power companies.

- **Standard & Poor's 500 Index** The S&P 500 consists of 500 companies, including 400 industrial, 20 transportation, 40 utility, and 40 financial companies. It is considered the broadest benchmark or market gauge for large-stock investors.

- **NASDAQ** There are two NASDAQ lists: NASDAQ National Market and NASDAQ Small-Cap Issues. They follow the performance of the stocks traded through the National Association of Securities Dealers Automated Quotation System. The NASDAQ National is comprised of the biggest companies that trade actively on NASDAQ. To be a component of this list, a company must meet certain SEC requirements such as market value, price, and volume. The NASDAQ Small-Cap list, as the name implies, is made up of smaller companies that also must meet certain requirements as dictated by NASDAQ itself. For instance, they must have at least two market-makers.

- **Russell Indexes** Compiled by Frank Russell Company in Tacoma, Washington, there are a number of Russell Indexes. The most popular ones include:

  The Russell 3000, the largest 3,000 U.S. stocks in terms of market capitalization. Stocks in this index have market caps ranging from $91 million to $85 billion.

  The Russell 1000, similar to the S & P 500, this index includes the highest ranking 1,000 stocks. Stocks in this index have an average market capitalization of about $4 billion.

  The Russell 2000 is made up of the other 2,000 stocks. The average market cap in this index is $255 million. This index is a good one to measure the performance of small cap stocks.

- **Wilshire 5000** This is the broadest stock market index, consisting of more than 5,000 common stocks traded on the NYSE, AMEX and OTC market.

- **EAFE Index** The EAFE Index (Morgan Stanley Index of European, Australian and Far East stocks) represents a composite of stocks in the stock markets in those three regions. It is a broad-based index used for tracking the performance of general international stocks.

- **Lipper General Equity Funds Average** This benchmark is compiled by Lipper Analytical Services, Inc., a mutual fund performance tracking firm. Using approximately 2,300 general equity mutual funds as its universe, it is an average total return for those funds for selected time periods.

Keeping an Eye on an Index   You should select an index or average that most closely reflects the kind of security you own. You can then track the performance of each on a regular basis by comparing percentage increases and decreases for specific periods of time. Record the percentage moves of an index next to those of your holdings at regular intervals.

There are many other indexes and averages besides those described above. You may want to read national business publications, such as the *Wall Street Journal* or *Barron's*, or check the business section of your local newspaper, to learn about less widely used or recognized benchmarks.

In this lesson, you learned about the most popular indexes and averages, how they are comprised, and how you can use them to track the performance of the stocks, or mutual funds you own.

Now that you've read the *10 Minute Guide to the Stock Market*, rest assured that you probably now know more about investing in the stock market than most of your friends. But don't stop there. Should you decide to invest in the stock market, take this knowledge, add to it, and hopefully—when it comes time for the counting—your investments will have rewarded you handsomely.

Good luck!

INDEX

T-Z